Minimum Impact Camping

A Basic Guide

Published by
Adventure Publications, Inc.
P. O. Box 269
Cambridge, MN 55008

Printed in the United States of America
ISBN: 0-934860-97-1

Cover Design Paula Roth
Illustrations by Paula Roth and Scott Zins
Photography by Leo McAvoy and Dan Seemon

Minimum Impact Camping

A Basic Guide

by
Curt Schatz
and
Dan Seemon

Dedication

Dr. Leo McAvoy (a professor at the University of Minnesota), Nevada Barr (now a ranger for the Park Service), and Wayne "Whitewater" Jastremski (our favorite kayaking fool) all provided inspiration, ideas, and support to the authors. We should, therefore, dedicate the book to them.

But, all things considered, we'd rather dedicate it to Buster, Lizzy, Harry, and the memory of Henri the cat.

Contents

Chapter 4: You'd Better Shop Around Some More

Chapter 5: And Such Small Portions!

Chapter 6: Under the Moon and Stars & Stuff

on knots), fires & firewood, lighting a fire, map & compass, if
you're lost, cleaning water, weather, loading your day pack, a
word on fishing

Chapter 7: Beyond the Pale

wood, fiberglass, plastic, Kevlar, aluminum

feathering, draw stroke, pry, J-stroke, ruddering, maine guide,
C-stroke

moving water, flatwater

special equipment, loading a pack, loading a canoe, care of the
canoe, portaging, choosing a campsite

Chapter 8: One Step Farther

Chapter 9: The Real Stuff?

Appendix

Introduction

Once upon a time, as all good stories must begin—we were hanging around with "the boys" talking about this, that and the other thing, and we somehow came up with a book title, "Under the Moon & Stars and stuff." We thought the title was so great, we wrote this book to go with it. Alas, while the publisher liked the book, he didn't like the title, and he asked us to change it. Our second try at a title was "The Almost Compleat Camper." Compleat because—like Isaac Walton, in the *Compleat Angler*—we do a bit of musing about the nature of the human experience, and *Almost*, because we aren't as good at it as Walton was. That title didn't go over too well, either, so eventually we settled on "Minimum Impact Camping." That, of course, is what the book's about.

In most respects, this book is a traditional camping guide. It contains enough information about camping equipment and techniques to help a beginning camper get started and an experienced camper go a bit farther. It also relates some of the attitudes and emotions shared by outdoor enthusiasts across time.

While none of the ideas we express here is really new, there is currency to the idea that the "natural" environments where we camp are precious and delicate, and that we need to treat them as carefully as we treat all the things we really value. The minimum impact camping movement recognizes this and acknowledges that no set of rules can completely govern our behavior towards the planet unless our attitudes make the rules a part of our nature.

We didn't invent this movement, but we are doing our best to contribute to it. We hope that by "spreading the word" we can do something to help protect the places we like best and to make time spent under the moon and stars a little more comfortable and enjoyable for others.

This book is intended to help you camp safely, with minimal impacts on the environment, yourself, and others. It isn't, however, intended to help you master the esoteric and complex skills needed for expeditions to very remote wilderness areas. It focuses on what we call front-woods camping, because that's what most people need; only practice and more formal education can help you develop the skills you need for more extended back-woods expeditions.

This is also a rule book. And, in spite of what we were told in child development classes, on "Oprah," and on "Donahue," we've included a number of rules that start with the word "don't," because we think that identifying the few things you shouldn't do is less restrictive than telling you exactly what you should do.

Finally, this book is supposed to be fun to read, so try not to get too serious on us.

The Authors

To better understand what we're saying, you'll want to know something about us before you read this book. Our opinions about camping behaviors and camping techniques necessarily reflect personal biases and experience, and are determined, to a large extent, by what we perceive and teach as being important. We're both teachers, and consequently, we often find it difficult to keep things simple.

We've both been Campers (with an upper-case "C") for pretty much our whole lives. As long as we can remember, we've been camping, reading and writing about camping, watching movies and television about camping, studying about camping, thinking about camping, and—not coincidentally—teaching other people about camping. You could call us camping addicts.

Curt studied English the first few years he was in college because he enjoyed reading while he was camping, and because he didn't know there was such a thing as a college degree program in outdoor recreation. Eventually, he discovered that he could study camping, so he did. He earned a master's degree in Outdoor Recreation/Education and a Ph.D. in Education. He's now a professor in the recreation program at New York's State University College at Cortland. Danny didn't study as much—he spent too much time camping, guiding trips, and selling equipment—but did manage to squeeze in a bachelor's degree in Environmental Studies and an M.A. in Outdoor Education/Recreation. He's now an environmental specialist with the Corps of Engineers.

The point here is, of course, that we both have a stamp of approval from a major Midwestern university (the University of Minnesota), in addition to loads of practical experience. Neither of us is a Paul Petzoldt, Harvey Manning, or My-Assistant-Jim (from Mutual of Omaha), and neither of us imagines we can have the public impact they've had; but we do know whereof we speak, and listening to our advice definitely isn't the worst thing you could do.

We've already mentioned that we hold some pretty strong beliefs about what camping is and what it isn't. We firmly believe that camping is, in every sense of the word, recreational. We believe, in fact, that it is the quintessential outdoor activity. But, because it's important for people to respect their environment and to pay attention to its needs as well as their own, we also believe that camping has to be governed by some pretty strict limitations on human behaviors. Showing respect, in our words and in our actions, for the natural environment, for other campers, and for ourselves can make camping a better experience for everyone and everything involved.

These better experiences are what the philosophy of minimum impact camping is all about.

Chapter 1

What's It All About?
An Introduction to Minimum Impact Camping

"Camping" is one of those ambiguous words that can mean a whole bunch of different things. In its most generic sense (the kind you'll find in a dictionary), the word *camping* seems to mean something like "voluntarily living in a tent or other temporary shelter for recreational reasons." In a more individualized sense, which is the only sense that really matters a whole lot, it seems that *camping* means something different to everyone.

When Dan and I refer to camping, we're usually working from a mental picture of ourselves perched atop a mountain in the wilds of Montana or cruising down the shore of Little Saganaga Lake in Minnesota's Boundary Waters Canoe Area. What we mean by camping, as it relates to our own lives, is something like minimum impact, human-powered travel through the wilderness. In contrast, a good friend of ours once told us that her idea of a real wilderness experience involved staying at a primitive facility–something like the Holiday Inn–in the same state as a National Park. When she refers to camping, she means staying in a motor home at a commercial campground with a heated pool and cable hookups.

Our point here, and there is a point, is that what you sleep in doesn't really define camping. Some *campers* take with them only what they can fit into a backpack and sleep on the bare ground. Some *campers* take whatever they can fit into a truck and sleep on a foam pad in a large tent. Some *campers* take an entire house (a motor home) along and sleep in a double bed under an electric blanket. What defines camping isn't as much physical as it is psychological.

1

Camping is a means of getting us away from our usual environment to a more primitive setting—one with less mechanization and worse plumbing. We use temporary shelters (like tents, trucks, or trailers) to remain mobile and get in closer contact with the out-of-doors and all the things that live there. Camping is sleeping under the moon and stars, cooking out on a tiny stove, and hiking a mountain trail; camping is also parking the R.V. in a campground and walking a well-groomed path. It's also fishing for bass and walleye, swimming in frigid water, lying in the sun at the beach, and a whole lot more.

Camping is an opportunity for us to spend more time caring for ourselves physically and psychologically, and an opportunity for us to take time to come to know ourselves better.

Camping is a chance to express our dreams and to practice being self-sufficient; it is an exercise in taking responsibility for ourselves and our own well being, away from the pressures, routines, and constraints of a mechanized society.

Camping is an opportunity to get closer to our environment and to learn to know its component parts through direct contact and physical involvement.

Camping is a chance to escape from anything we don't like about our lives and a chance to grow beyond those things so it doesn't matter any more if we like or dislike them.

More than anything else, camping is a chance for us to find out where it is we fit in this world.

We like to picture the earth as a closed system, just like the mayonnaise-jar terrarium we made in the fifth grade. Energy flows through this system in a loop. It starts at the sun, of course, but once it reaches the planet, energy flows from plants, to animals, to the earth itself, and then back to plants in a continuous cycle. This cycle is what makes the planet alive, and also what keeps it healthy.

We humans—in a metaphorical sense, at least—often picture ourselves as residing outside "the jar." We look at the environments in which we live as something apart from the *natural* environment, rather than seeing ourselves and our communities as a component of that natural environment.

2

Camping is a special form of recreation because it helps us to realize we are actually inside "the jar." (At least Curt and I like to think it does.) Consequently, camping can help us be more aware of the cycles of the "real" world. It can also help us to learn emotionally, as well as intellectually, that ignoring the closed nature of our planet's ecological cycle is, sooner or later, going to ruin the terrarium. In this sense, camping is not only an activity, it is also an attitude of respect and concern for the natural environment.

We would like to add that camping is not an opportunity to live off the land without any rules or inhibitions—as we often imagine our forefathers and foremothers did. Camping allows an escape from the rules and regulations of modern society; but it is, and must be, governed by an ethic of its own.

While this book is partly about camping equipment and partly about camping techniques, it is mostly about that ethic. If you can learn *why* we like camping by reading this book, then you'll understand our attitude toward the environment. We think that is the hardest thing to learn about camping.

Minimum Impact Recreation

One of the growing movements in wilderness recreation is called minimum impact camping. Minimum impact is just what it claims to be. Its object is to minimize the social and environmental impacts the camper has on her or his chosen recreational environment. While minimum impact camping evolved from a need to protect the delicate ecosystems of North America's wilderness areas, it is important to extend the idea of minimum impact camping to all your outdoor recreation activities. That is, in order to maintain the variety of pleasant options that has dragged you away from your refrigerator and VCR remote control, it is important that you practice minimum impact recreation.

Because you are really interested in camping, the outdoors has some appeal for you. In order to maintain that appeal in the future, it is necessary to preserve the characteristics in the environment that are appealing. Since we don't always know what those characteristics are, it is a good idea to take a conservative position and to preserve the physical and social environments of a recreational experience to the greatest degree possible. What all of this comes down to, in the simplest terms, is this:

1. Don't hurt yourself.
2. Don't trash the environment.
3. Don't bother anyone else.

Three Kinds of Impact

Any activity in which you participate—including camping—can have an impact on you, the environment, and on others. You should be aware of what those impacts are and work hard to minimize the negative aspects of all of them.

It is important to minimize negative impacts on yourself because you want, it is reasonable to assume, to enjoy yourself; and negative impacts don't usually make for a good time. You can best minimize impact on yourself by planning what you are doing, or what you're going to do, by not exceeding your ability level and by being careful.

It is important to minimize your impacts on the environment for much the same reason. Damaging the environment is not, or should not be, a "good time." We believe that the land-community (the flora and fauna that inhabit the places we camp) has rights and that you are obliged to minimize your impact on it simply because it is. Even if you don't share this belief, you should minimize your environmental impact anyway because if you don't, you won't be able to continue enjoying the environment.

Minimizing your negative impacts on others is important because "they" want to have fun too. We admit that minimizing impacts on others isn't always easy, and some people behave in a manner that just calls out for maximum impacts like a right hook to the jaw. We believe, nonetheless, that common courtesy dictates minimizing social impacts. So show a bit of consideration for others' needs, wants, and rights, and place yourself (metaphorically) in your neighbors' sleeping bags before you get the guitars out at midnight.

What's It All About?

This book emphasizes an attitude towards the outdoors as well as techniques to help you meet these three goals, minimizing your impact on yourself, the environment, and others, while still having fun. Even this guide, though, doesn't (and can't) provide a comprehensive explanation of everything you can do to minimize your impact. You will need to figure out for yourself what is right and what isn't in many situations. The only way you can accomplish that is to adopt a minimum impact philosophy and to constantly try to modify your behavior to fit that philosophy. Believing that you can minimize your impact on others without diminishing your own experience can help you to decide what's right and what isn't.

There are some key points we want you to consider and we've included them in a brief quiz. So, get out your pencil, make sure it has a good point, and answer the following questions.

Minimum Impact Camping Quiz

Section 1
True/False Questions

T F   1. It is a good idea to use brightly colored tents so your campsite can be easily spotted in an emergency.

T F   2. One should burn and then bury used cans and other metal containers.

T F   3. The size of a camping group is unimportant.

T F   4. Meadows and grassy areas are usually the preferred place to camp in a wilderness or primitive area.

T F   5. To avoid excessive damage to the environment, stay no more than two days at one campsite.

T F   6. It's always a good idea to build a circle of stones to contain a campfire.

T F   7. A minimum impact site should be at least 200 feet from trails, lakes, streams, meadows, or scenic areas.

T F   8. A cat-hole latrine should be dug in dry, sandy, or gravel soil, at least 50 feet from water, camp, or trails.

T F   9. Fish entrails should be tossed back into the lake or stream as food for turtles and other fish.

T F   10. Loud games and campfire programs are appropriate camping activities for large groups.

T F   11. If conditions are muddy, it is a good idea to walk beside and parallel to the established trail.

T F 12. It is good etiquette to leave a pile of wood for the next user of a primitive site.

T F 13. Rules don't apply in the wilderness.

Section 2
Other Questions

1. Besides hanging your food pack properly, what is the best way to avoid problems with bears at your site?

2. Why should you wear lightweight shoes at your campsite?

3. What key words describe the most appropriate type of wood for use in your cooking fire?

4. What is the best way to dispose of food scraps?

5. Describe an ideal tent site.

6. Why should you not build fires directly on the ground?

7. Is bark peeled from a live birch tree a good form of tinder?

8. How can you tell if your fire is completely out?

9. Describe the best procedure for washing anything (including yourself) with soap in a wilderness area.

10. Describe a no-trace check.

11. How large an axe is required for safe camping?

12. What does "take nothing but pictures, leave nothing but footprints" mean?

We've included brief answers to these questions at the end of the book (for those of you who just can't wait to check your work), but since we know that you're interested in more than brief answers, we've also included more detailed discussions in the next eight chapters.

The book is, more or less, laid out in the order in which you would have to undertake each activity if you were actually going on a camping trip. Chapter 2 focuses on pretrip planning, our rules for camping safety, and contains a few comments about timing for your camping trip. Chapter 3 provides as much detail as we dare provide about camping equipment, and Chapter 4 includes similar details about camping clothes and materials (along with fashion tips). Chapter 5, one of our favorites, deals with food, cooking, and because of our concern for ourselves, nutrition. Minimum impact camping techniques are detailed in Chapter 6, by which time you will be actually camping. Much of what we know about canoes and canoeing is in Chapter 7, and a basic guide to hiking and backpacking makes up Chapter 8. Chapter 9 is our last attempt to explicate our philosophies of camping and also includes a few comments about how to go about heading for the woods. We follow all this with a collection of checklists (equipment and clothes), a sample menu, and finally, the answers to our camping quiz.

Chapter 2

Safety, Time, and Space
Tips on Planning a Camping Trip

It is important for you to plan your camping experiences. In fact, we both think it is so important, we are willing to predict that not planning your trips will almost certainly result in your having a very bad time. If you do plan your trips, however, you have reason to hope for mostly good experiences. Careful planners offer the most potential for becoming repeat campers.

We are adamant that planning is an essential first step. We really are. Really!

This is not to say that you need to schedule every minute of your camping trips. Planning and scheduling are as different as alligators and crocodiles; while the two should never be confused, they are often mistaken for each other. Planning deals with the wide (like an alligator's nose) sweep of events related to camping, while scheduling relates to the narrow (like a croc's snout) focus of each hour on "the trail." There is no reason to schedule every minute and detail of your trip; indeed, there are lots of reasons not to do so, but you've really got to plan. Fortunately you can plan a trip quite quickly once you've had some practice.

The things you have to consider in planning are safety, time, equipment, food, and clothing. These rather broad categories apply regardless of where you are going to camp. Scheduling, which you don't need to do carefully in advance, will depend on the merits of the specific place you choose to camp (we hope it has a place for you to hang a small hammock), your mood once you get there, and the weather.

Safety

We should start this section by stating emphatically that your safety is always your own responsibility—and we shall.

Your safety is always your own responsibility!

Despite the incredible number of liability suits reported in the press that might suggest otherwise, you can't expect anyone else—a companion, a group leader, or the park service—to accept responsibility for you under normal conditions. In order to be safe, you must assume responsibility for yourself.

To take responsibility for yourself, you have to know your limits—that is, you need to know what you are and are not capable of doing. An honest self-evaluation is the best way for you to determine that what you are choosing to do is safe, *for you*, and we might add, for the people with whom you are doing it.

You also have to be aware that physical limits and psychological limits are different. Physical limits refer, not surprisingly, to what you are physically capable of doing. Psychological limits refer to what feels, in an emotional sense, okay for you to do. Physical and psychological limits are not entirely unrelated, but it is best for the beginner to think of them as separate things.

Do not let your psychological desires outreach your physical abilities. You may, for example, decide you want to do some major whitewater as part of your first canoeing experience. This might not present a problem psychologically—if you don't have a thing about cold water, big waves, and potential death—but physically you can be almost certain you're asking for trouble. In hikers' terms, what we're saying is that if you are physically capable of no more than a short hike, don't try to carry a *stone* (a trendy term for a loaded backpack) up a mountain.

The inverse of this relationship also holds true. If you are healthy and have sufficient skills to make you *physically* capable of camping in the cold, dark, wild woods, don't feel obligated to stray too far from the comforts of a lighted washroom if you're not feeling adventuresome. Regardless of your physical abilities, there is no shame in admitting that all you are equipped for, *psychologically*, is an afternoon with a good novel and a beach chair.

Safety rule number one, then, is to determine what you can and cannot do before you do anything else. And safety rule number two is to not do anything for which you are unprepared either physically or psychologically.

Our safety rule number three is to take whatever time you need to learn any required skills before you start an activity. This might involve reading a guide book (just like this one) to be prepared for a basic camping adventure, attending a five-week course on mountaineering to do some serious mountain climbing, or earning a Ph.D. to get paid to talk about it. Whatever it takes for you to feel comfortable and to be physically safe, do it.

Rule four is to promise yourself, and anyone who cares about you), that you'll stop whatever you're doing as soon as it reaches the limits of your skill, knowledge, comfort, and training. If you can't keep this promise, stay at home. Although we've always been real lucky and have managed to escape our own stupidity mostly intact, we can make this assertion from experience. There are times we've ignored this rule and suffered some ensuing pain as a result.

One of us admits that the worst injury he's ever suffered by exceeding his ability and training is a mildly sprained ankle and some seriously bruised pride; Dan, on the other hand, claims to have never hurt himself (although Curt can remember at least one time when Dan stupidly, but not seriously, injured his shoulder). Both of us have been lucky. A lot of beginners have been hurt, or killed, because they thought they could do things they knew nothing about. Injuring yourself is not a minimum impact activity.

Even experienced campers, including us, will privately admit to one or two stupid injuries that they won't acknowledge in public. Injured pride sometimes hurts more than injured bodies.

Anyway—to skillfully change the subject—safety rule number five is to check your equipment carefully before starting a trip. Make sure it all works, is in good condition, and is all there (i.e., don't forget the toilet paper). Make sure it's the right equipment, too. On one trip we mistakenly took a rather small sleeping bag for a rather large man. It was cold, uncomfortable, and unnecessary.

Be sure, (rule six) that you know how to use what you carry. A camping stove will only cook your food if it works. If you can't get it to light, it's three pounds of garbage. Even worse, if you use a stove incorrectly it becomes three pounds of potential disaster.

Rule seven is to let someone know where you are going and when they can expect you back. Tell your neighbor, your parents, a park ranger, or anyone else who will be able to call the county sheriff if you don't come home on time. Remember to let this person know when you do come back on schedule, so they don't get worried and call out the hounds for nothing. A brief summary of the rules thus far:

1. determine what you can and can't do before you do anything else;

2. don't do anything for which you are physically or psychologically unprepared;

3. take whatever time you need to learn the necessary skills before you start an activity;

4. promise yourself, and anyone who cares about you, that you'll stop whatever it is you are doing as soon as it reaches the limits of your skill and knowledge;

5. check your equipment carefully before starting a trip;

6. make sure that you know how to use the equipment you carry; and,

7. always let someone know where you are going and when they can expect you back.

There are a whole bunch of other aspects to camping safety that you should consider. Many of them, like the rules for rock climbing and glacier work, are so complex that they require books and classes of their own. Others, like be careful with sharp knives, are part of everyday life. A few items, however, do merit specific mention.

Before you go camping you ought to know something about (1) the weather; be aware of what it is and what it is becoming. Check on the weather reports wherever you are and pay attention to what is going on around you; (2) site specific hazards; the managers of whatever resource you use should have some information on things like tainted water supplies and various hazards in the terrain (sink holes, hidden waterfalls, windfalls over trails and the like). Dealing with problems like these requires up-to-date information that can best be provided on site; (3) first aid; take a class from the American Red Cross or any similar organization—it's well worth the time and energy; and, (4) specific animal hazards; these will vary with the resource you use, and current information on bears that have been raiding campsites, rogue chipmunks, or local skunk populations will prevent any surprises. Also, pay attention to such things as hunting regulations and seasons. Do you really want to be in the woods during deer season? We'll add that it's important to leave your large knives, axes, guns, and other totally unnecessary and potentially dangerous tools at home.

We can't address every aspect of safety here so just keep in mind that safety in the woods isn't (or shouldn't be) that different from safety in the home. Everything you know about living at home applies to camping, too. Scrapes and bruises will result from falls in the woods or on the street, animal bites are dangerous in any environment, food is almost always good for your body, personal hygiene is always important, throwing lighted things on the floor can start a fire, and so on, and so on, and so on. The biggest difference between home and camping is that when you're camping, you will be farther from your closet, your bank, and the phone—and from the help these amenities can provide.

Time

Time planning starts with deciding how long you will be gone on your trip—a prerequisite for buying enough food to last through the experience and for letting a friend or family member know when to call out the search parties. When you plan *time quantity*, consider time quality as well. *When* you are going outdoors has an influence on what you'll find when you get there.

Time of year is a prime consideration. In most parts of the U.S. (and more than a few places in Canada), everyone, and their in-laws, takes to the woods at certain times: the weekend after school lets out, the week before it starts back, Independence Day (known on Minnesota's "range" as *Fort-July*), Canada Day (commonly known as 1 July), and the first weekend in August. Because these times are so popular, you might be hard pressed to find a campsite, or even a hotel room, over any of these weekends without advance reservations. On the other hand, mid-January tends to be rather uncrowded in most northern campgrounds, which makes finding a tent site easy, although you might find sunbathing in three feet of snow just a little bit uncomfortable. If you think crowds and excessive cold might diminish the quality of your experience plan to avoid them both.

While it is easier to find a site and to minimize your impacts if you avoid the camping rush hours, it's not necessary to avoid summer altogether; just pick an off weekend. Consider starting your trip midweek, as Wednesday and Thursday aren't as crowded as the weekends.

Time of day is also an important consideration when you plan the beginning of your trip. If you leave for the campground (or wilderness area, or backyard) after work, you are likely to get there after dark. It's hard to set up camp with no light, especially if the park is full and/or closed when you get there. Also, in the event that you do find a site after dark, using headlights and bright lanterns is rude and likely to disturb the campground's other residents (human and not). Enough said? Leaving for your trip early in the day, when you are well rested, makes the drive safer. Make camp before dark and you're setting yourself up for a better, higher quality experience.

If your camping trip will include activities like canoeing or hiking, it is important for you to plan carefully how far you can go in a day. Remember that the terrain and your experience will both have a big influence on this distance. While it is easy for an experienced hiker to walk 15 miles a day on level ground with a full pack, that distance might be difficult for a city slicker who never walks much, regardless of the weight of his or her pack, or impossible, even for an experienced packer, on a rough mountainous trail. Planning *time on trail*, then, requires you to know where you are going and how well you can deal with the geography of the place.

The time on trail should also be flexible. Consider planning alternate routes or optional loops to shorten or lengthen your trip if necessary. Even if your hikes or paddles are only day trips, make sure you plan enough time for rest stops and lunch, and be sure you don't go so far that you can't get home or to camp before sunset.

If you'll permit us to do so, we'd like to interject a pointed tale at this point.

A friend of ours, a fellow canoe guide, failed to plan his time on trail effectively. He was guiding a group of teenage boys and began to cross a nasty, long portage (a trail of dubious quality between two lakes) too late in the day and became stuck halfway through. Normally, this wouldn't be a problem as it's easy to camp on a portage if it's dry. This one, though, was a swamp. He had no alternative but to sleep in the swamp and finish up the next morning. No one was hurt, but we can imagine sleeping in a swamp was not a high-quality experience.

Finally, to close our comments on chronology, plan plenty of *time for rest* and sleep. Keeping well-rested and alert is vital to your safety and should be an important consideration in any time plan. Enough sleep can also make a vacation, even a camping one, much more recreational; when you're on vacation, you shouldn't have to reach the summit to have fun.

Space

Where you camp, like when you camp, directly affects the quality of your experience. Try to pick a camping area that you know something about, and if possible, one that you know you enjoy. Also, camp somewhere that is intended for camping. People often get very upset if you camp on private property without permission, and government agencies get just as upset if you camp on public land dedicated to some other activity.

State Parks, State Forests, National Parks, and National Recreation Areas generally are good places to camp (as are some private campgrounds and not a few other public places). If you pick one of these, you can make reservations in advance, and you can almost certainly be assured of a variety of recreational opportunities.

Another Note on Planning

We mentioned, just a few pages ago, that planning needs to take into account your safety, time, food, equipment, and clothes. We have provided a few general guidelines for planning, indicated how closely these categories are interrelated, and looked at the first two categories. The categories we haven't dealt with yet (food, clothes, and equipment) each need more than a few paragraphs of explanation, and therefore get chapters of their own. None of these topics are more important than safety and time planning (as the individual chapters might suggest), they just take more time to explain.

Chapter 3

You'd Better Shop Around
Camping Equipment

Most of the readily available books on camping equipment seem to deal with expedition or backwoods (almost-expedition) quality gear, and most of the once-great catalogues now seem to focus almost exclusively on clothes and expedition gear. We both like yuppie pseudo-country clothes, and we can't deny the advantages of ultra high-quality, lightweight camping gear designed for living in the outdoors for extended periods. Nonetheless, we suggest that not everyone needs them. Only the equipment companies and our gear-head friends might disagree.

Expedition quality equipment—gear that is suitable for extended wilderness trips—is usually expensive and far exceeds most people's needs. If you are camping out of a car, or a relatively short distance from one, somewhat heavier, less expensive, and less specialized equipment should serve you just as well. High quality is always important, though, because it helps to insure (among other things) hassle free, or at least minimum hassle, camping.

Transportation

The equipment you need for basic camping starts with a means of transportation. We are not trying to create controversy here, but we will be expressing a bias in favor of the car.

Bicycle trips are great fun, but they require more specific information than we're providing here and the ultralight, specialized equipment they demand is expensive. Motorcycles can be fun, too, but they can also be dangerous (we ride, we know); so unless you are an experienced rider, you shouldn't use one for camping. Also, you can't carry a canoe or full backpack on a bike of either type.

Yuppie Urban Assault Vehicles—overpowered four-wheel-drive trucks—are gas hogs and tempt people to drive places they shouldn't drive. Since we want to minimize impacts, we try to avoid such temptations. All things considered, we have to recommend against such vehicles.

Our favorite means of transport, as we've already hinted, is a basic, little, high-mileage car. Cars work really well; they'll take you most places you need to go, offering a sense of freedom without doing too much damage to the environment.

No matter what mode of transport you choose, getting to and from the park or other locale where you'll be camping is almost surely the most dangerous part of a camping trip. Once you settle this transportation issue, more specialized equipment becomes important.

Basic Equipment Needs

Most of the gear you'll ever need to camp successfully is included in our basic equipment list. This is a very general list, and it is likely that it will not be exactly suited to your needs. It is a good shopping guide, though, and should certainly get you started.

Basic Equipment for Overnight Camping
(Summer Conditions)

Group Equipment (for 4–6 people)

The Kitchen

stove/s: 2 one-burner models
fuel for stove: 1 liter/stove/day (2 hot meals)
pour spout or funnel for fuel
pots & pans: minimum of 1-qt. & 2-qt.
pots with lids, frying pan & lid
coffee pot & lid (never forget this)
pliers or pot gripper
mixing spoon & spatula
lighter &/or matches
water filter (if no potable water source is available)

water bladder or jug
food bags
food (enough for 3 meals/person/day for the whole trip)
50'–100' lightweight nylon rope (usually 1/4")
garbage bag
pot scrubber (nylon)
some form of towel (helpful, but not essential)
spice kit

The Campsite

tarp (waterproof)

trowel (if no toilets &/or washing areas are available at campground)

tents with poles & stakes (enough room for everyone in your party)

first-aid kit (a basic list of contents is provided below)

repair kit (for tent, clothes, stove, etc.)

toilet paper

candle lantern (& extra candles)

emergency food & shelter (for overnight trips)

individual equipment (for 1 person)

Essential Equipment

closed-cell or nylon-coated foam pad (for sleeping)

sleeping bag (& stuff sack)

map/s & compass (also know how to use them!)

whistle

small pocket knife (adults only)

water bottle

cup, bowl, spoon, knife, fork, plate

toilet articles (including a towel or large bandana, hand lotion, toothbrush & paste, lip balm, biodegradable soap, tampons or sanitary napkins, lighter)

sunglasses

sunscreen

flashlight (not a bad idea to carry extra batteries)

day pack or fanny-pack (optional)

insect repellent

sit pad

Luxury Items–May Be Essential

pillow (we hate to leave home without one)

small folding chair (a canoe seat works well)

solar shower

hammock

books

Optional Equipment

fishing gear	camera & film	cards
games	harmonica	walking stick
bear bell	diary & pencil	notebook
binoculars	watch or travel alarm	thermometer (air temp)
field guides (birds, plants, insects, animals)		

You probably already have some of this equipment and can easily find much of the rest at local garage sales or thrift stores. Some of it, though, is hard to find outside outdoor specialty stores. We'd suggest that you do some comparison shopping before you make any major purchases. When, or if, your mama told you, "You'd better shop around," she was right, because if you don't you might end up with an outrageous bill from the local outdoor store. Quality doesn't come cheap, but sometimes it's cheaper one place than another.

The more expensive specialty items from this list (stoves, sleeping bags, tents, and their ilk) are usually available for rent. Check your local phone directory before you shop around too much, and you might be able to save a few dollars by renting, rather than buying, a few things.

As with everything else, we have strong opinions about what is good, bad, necessary, and unnecessary equipment. What follows is as close as we can come to an unbiased, but ideologically correct, expression of what constitutes real essential camping equipment.

While we have no particular desire to endorse any one manufacturer's or stores products over another, we do cite name brands in the discussion of equipment below. We're not trying to say, implicitly or explicitly, that the products we mention are the best; they're just the ones with which we are both familiar and pleased. Talk to salespeople, friends, relatives, and neighbors about equipment (or rent different kinds and try them out), and decide what is best *for you* before you buy any product.

Equipment Specifics

Stoves

We always cook on a stove when we are camping. We do so because very few places where large numbers of people camp in the U.S. or Canada can replenish wood supplies as fast as campers can burn them, and because stoves are less likely than fires to scar the land or burn the forest. We strongly suggest that you, too, use a stove when camping out. Good ones are available from about $30 to $100. A maintenance/repair kit ($6 and up) should be purchased with most stoves (unless you are real optimistic).

Anyone who has ever cooked a serious meal should understand why we like to have at least two burners. One holds the coffee pot, the second the soup. We prefer to get these two burners by using two one-burner stoves, rather than one two-burner. This makes it possible for us to spread out our kitchen enough so that two people can cook comfortably, and makes it easy for us to take one lightweight stove along on day trips; we often like to have a hot drink at lunchtime. If you use small one-burner stoves, it is

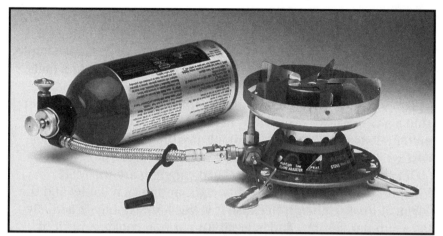

One Burner Stove—Photo Courtesy of Coleman Company, Inc.

also easy to move from car camping to such atavistic activities as backpacking and canoe tripping without investing in new equipment. Coleman, MSR, Optimus, Svea, and a number of other manufacturers make good small stoves. If you want to get a two-burner or larger stove, you'll find your options—in manufacturer, as well as in use—are more restricted. A number of good multiburner stoves are on the market, but most of them seem to be made by Coleman.

As for fuel, you'll find there are almost as many possibilities as there are stove manufacturers. The most common fuels seem to be kerosene, butane, alcohol, and the various forms of gasoline. Alcohol, and the occasional candle-powered stoves work, but tend to be slow, especially those candle ones; they don't produce as much heat as the stoves that deliver vaporized fuel under pressure. Kerosene stoves work fine, and kerosene is a readily available fuel, but we find it too messy to bother with. Butane stoves work very well, but generally use non-reusable fuel canisters. That makes them somewhat expensive to operate, annoying to carry on extended trips, and increases their long-term impact on the environment. Propane (or LPG) stoves can use refillable canisters, but the canisters weigh so much, we only use them at home. White-gas stoves are the most common, and we prefer them over the others.

If you are willing to invest some extra money (though the extra amount seems to grow smaller every year), or are planning on traveling outside the U.S. or Canada, you can, and perhaps should, buy a stove that will burn more than one of these common fuels. We once met a man who claimed his multi-fuel stove, an MSR X-GK™, would burn a mixture of spit and Kool-aid™ at 12,000 feet (that's altitude). We doubt that his story was true, but a good multi-fuel stove will burn just about anything flammable (or at least white gas, unleaded gasoline and/or kerosene).

Our favorite stoves for general-use camping are the MSR WhisperLite™, because it is lightweight and very reliable; and the Coleman Peak 1 Apex™, because it is very adjustable (it actually has a simmer setting) and is great for serious cooking. Both of these stoves use white gas, but both also come in multi-fuel models.

Pots, Pans, & Other Utensils

When just the two of us go camping, we carry a coffee pot, a small frying pan, a 1¹/₂-quart and a 1-quart pot, and lids for all of them. If we have four or five people, we add an extra 2-quart kettle. When we're fishing, we also take two frying pans, one for fish and one for spuds. Whatever your preference, it is important to carry something better than a Boy Scout mess kit to cook in if you plan on eating well.

Nesting pot sets are readily available at most outdoor equipment stores for $20 and up; some of them are designed for use with a specific stove, and others are for more generic use. They also come in a variety of materials and sizes. If you are buying pots, it is a good idea to remember that any pot that holds water is better than one that doesn't and that small stoves work best with small pots. While it is not necessary for you to buy a set of pots specially designed for a particular stove, it might not be a bad idea to buy a set designed to nest for easy and compact packing. You might also consider getting a coffee pot that is big enough to hold your stove so you can take both (the pot and stove, that is) along on day hikes to make tea or coffee at teatime without wasting a lot of space in your day pack.

The most common materials for camping cookware include alu-

Stainless Steel Set—Photo Courtesy of Coleman Company, Inc.

minum, stainless steel, cast iron, and enameled steel. Aluminum pots generally seem to be the least expensive. They weigh less than cast-iron and enameled pots, they tend to be durable, and they are easy to find. Stainless is very durable, not *too* heavy, easy to clean, and readily available in outdoor specialty stores. Cast iron is readily available, but is too heavy to use away from the car; and enamel, while it is pretty, is also heavy and is prone to chipping with the kind of use we give it. A decent set of aluminum or stainless cookware is a good investment.

If you opt for an aluminum set, you might want to consider using a coated frying pan; the non-stick bottoms make cooking and cleaning much easier. Lids, for all of your pots and pans, are also important if you want to keep grit out of your food and heat in it.

We both have small, nesting, stainless pot sets and can recommend both Peak 1™ by Coleman and Evernew™ products.

Any good spatula and mixing/serving spoon will work as well when camping as they do at home. We do recommend light aluminum or polycarbonate ones, though, because the cheap plastic utensils melt—or get real, real soft—when hot, and wood implements are hard to keep clean. A pot scrubber (one of those little nylon jobs, not your spouse) is also a must.

Unless your hands are impervious to heat, you will need some sort of handle for your pots and pans. Most camping pots don't come equipped with built-in ones. If they did, they wouldn't nest and would be hard to fit into a full pack. You will, therefore, need either a pot gripper (one will come with most sets of camping cookware) or a pair of pliers. We recommend the latter because pliers are also useful when you are repairing equipment.

For minimum impact reasons, we don't build fires anymore, but we do carry lighters to light our stoves and candle lantern. We generally use a lighter rather than matches, because matches are often more trouble than they are worth and lighters work (sort of) even when they're wet. We do make a point of carrying waterproof and/or carefully packaged matches in a pocket and in several different places in our packs, though, because lighters aren't always reliable. We'd also like to join the manufacturers in recommending that you don't carry a disposable lighter in your shirt pocket because there have been reports of them blowing up unexpectedly.

Food bags—either plastic bags or coated nylon stuff sacks—are a good way of keeping your food dry and organized. We use a separate bag for each of the day's meals, breakfast, lunch, and dinner. Inside our large meal bags, we carry individual meals packed in reusable plastic bags or containers. This system requires that we spend a few hours preparing food for our trips, but it makes cooking on trail a whole lot easier and more organized.

The last vital piece of equipment in your kitchen is your garbage bag. You need one even if you cook on a fire because plastic, metal (including aluminum foil), and leftover food don't burn. "Carry out everything you carry in" is a good rule to follow and includes your camping kitchen. We generally spend a few minutes picking up other people's litter in every campsite we use and end up carrying out more than we carried in. Almost any bag will serve effectively as a garbage bag, and any bag is surely better than none.

Rope

Rope is very important to most campers. You can use rope for so many things—clotheslines, anchor lines, tarp lines, hanging food, tying down boats, holding up tents or pants (if you lose a belt), and an almost infinite range of other neat things. Ropes, like everything else, come in a variety of sizes and materials. For general use, we avoid natural fibers and polyester; they work fine, but are often hard to untie. Nylon parachute cord is lightweight and will serve for most purposes, like hanging a tarp between trees— so you have a dry place to cook and eat if it rains. Heavier rope is necessary, though, if you need to hang your food bags at night or tie down a boat. We always carry two 50-foot coils of extra parachute cord and one or two 25-foot coils of quarter-inch braided nylon rope with the kitchen equipment, just because they are so very useful.

Water Supply

In most developed campgrounds, pumps or faucets will provide you with easy access to a safe source of water for drinking and cooking. If no such facilities are available, you will need to carry something that can be used to treat your water. In a very few undeveloped places, you can safely drink water taken straight from a lake (from under the surface, at least 100 feet from shore) or streams, but because most untreated water sources in the U.S. are not clean enough to drink safely, we recommend that you boil, chemically treat, or filter all the water you don't get out of a spigot.

This is important because of the very common little giardia cyst. When this water-borne parasite lodges in a human intestine, it takes about ten days to develop into an active protozoan and reproduce enough to cause a variety of problems including explosive diarrhea, cramps, flatulence, and a whole range of related discomforts. Giardiasis, or "beaver-fever," is not fun. Boiling, filtering, and chemically treating water can prevent giardiasis, and can also remove bacterial contaminants (like fecal coliform bacteria) from your water supply. They are, consequently, a good way to avoid some of the most common causes of diarrhea.

We both think boiling water is too time and fuel consuming to be practical, so we try to avoid it ourselves. It is probably the least expensive alternative, though, because all it requires is the stove and pot you use for cooking.

Chemical treatments (about $2 and up) usually use some form

of chlorine, which will kill bacteria and should kill protozoa and other microscopic parasites (like giardia cysts), or iodine, which will kill both bacteria and protozoa. Unfortunately, both chlorine and iodine can leave an awful taste in the water.

Unlike boiling and chemical treatments, filtering water can remove particular pollutants—naturally occurring mud and little bugs that aren't really pollutants at all but do look gross—as well as bacteria, protozoa, and other microscopic parasites. If the filter has a carbon element, it will remove some organic chemicals. If it has an iodine element, it will also remove viral contaminant's. If you are concerned about viral contaminant's and don't have a filter that incorporates iodine in its filtration system, you'll have to treat your water with iodine and then filter it. Good filters for personal or small-group use range in price from about $30 to $200.

We've tried a variety of filters including the First Need™, Katadyn Pocket Filter™, MSR WaterWorks™, Pur Explorer Water

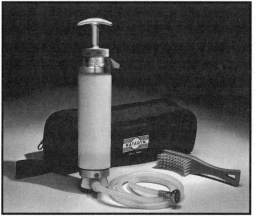

Purifier™, and Water I™, and all of them worked well enough. Because the differences in prices between filters seem to correlate with the output and ease of use, the more you pay, the happier you might be if you want water in a hurry. The more expensive filters ($100 and up) are wonderful. The MSR Waterworks™, for exam-

Water Filter Kit—Photo courtesy of Katadyn U. S. A., Inc.

ple, is easy to use and has a four-stage filter, including carbon, to remove bacteria, protozoa, and organic chemicals. The Pur™ filter (another of the more expensive ones) is the only backcountry filter we're aware of that incorporates iodine directly into its filtration system to remove viruses, and it's great, too. On the other hand, the First Need™, which both of us use, is relatively inexpensive, is as effective as most of the expensive models, and is only a little bit more awkward to use.

A water bladder or jug that holds at least three gallons can make cooking and eating in camp a lot easier. Using a bladder can save you numerous trips to your source of water in the middle of a meal and will provide you an opportunity to carry large amounts of potable water with you, in a boat, car, or canoe, during any extended day trips. If you're interested in a really convenient system, MSR's Dromedary™ bags connect directly to their filter, and the First Need™ can connect directly to a wide-mouthed Nalgene™ water bottle.

Tarpaulins

Tarps are versatile accessories. We like to carry one tarp with the kitchen equipment so we have a dry place to eat, and a second tarpaulin for use as a "ground cloth" to help keep us clean and dry inside the tent in very wet weather or to put our sleeping pads on if it's nice enough to sleep without a tent. We also use a tarp to protect our equipment at night.

Tarps range upward in price from about $5 and come in a variety of materials. The most common seem to be nylon, plastic, and canvas. Nylon is lightweight and packs easily, and it can be manufactured with polyurethane coating which makes it very waterproof, and reinforcing threads, which make it rip resistant. Canvas tends to be heavy, but it can be waterproof, is highly resistant to sunlight (nylon does deteriorate after a few years of use) and abrasion, and lasts for years. Plastic, while it can be made rip resistant (just like rip-stop nylon), is not very durable, but it is inexpensive. We prefer coated nylon tarps because they are much more durable than plastic ones, are just as waterproof as canvas or plastic, and are much more versatile than either of the others; and they usually come with metal grommets in the corners. They're also lightweight and easy to pack.

Tents

You can buy a cheap tent for about $15, but the good ones range from about $80 to $600. Eureka, Diamond, Sierra Designs, REI (Recreational Equipment, Inc.), EMS (Eastern Mountain Sports), North Face, and Moss all make good tents.

Dome
Rainfly not shown

A-Frame

Tents, like tarps, come in a variety of materials. Almost all of them offer some advantages, and none is perfect for all conditions. Nylon, though, is an extremely versatile material. It has a high strength-to-weight ratio, packs compactly, and dries quickly, making it a very good choice for tents. Nylon, though, is not perfect. It melts when exposed to high temperatures, like open flames, so it is very important to be careful with fire around nylon tents; and it will break down after years of use from exposure to the sun, so even nylon tents won't last forever.

Two kinds of material (waterproof and water-permeable) are, or at least, should be, used in manufacturing nylon tents. The floor and rain fly of any good nylon tent should be waterproofed, but the tent walls should not. Everyone expels moisture during the night (and the day too) through sweat and through respiration. If the tent walls are not gas permeable, moisture will collect inside the tent like dew. A tent with uncoated nylon walls lets this vapor escape and dissipate outside where it belongs. A waterproof rain fly outside the tent is necessary to keep rain out. When shopping for a tent, keep this in mind.

A number of tents are now being made from breathable waterproof materials, like Gore-Tex™. They seem to work very well and weigh next to nothing. They are also, or so some say, less flame resistant than treated nylon or canvas. On the average, they also cost a lot. We don't object to improved materials, but if you don't need ultra-light equipment, you're probably better off staying with lower-tech materials.

A tent's design depends on its purpose. Because we believe our tent is a good place to sleep but not too good a place for anything else, we're happy with a small one that provides about 15 to 20 square feet of floor space per person, with little else in the form of accessories. If you intend to spend time in a tent playing games or watching television, you'll need a taller tent (one you can stand in, like a large A-frame) that provides 20 or more square feet/person, and you should consider luxury additions like vestibules and double doors.

Some tents need to be completely staked out and roped up to keep their shape, and some (the self-standing ones) have poles that attach to the tent so they keep their shape, or most of it, anyway without ropes or stakes. This isn't a major consideration unless you plan on camping on rock or permafrost, but for convenience's sake, you'll probably want to consider a self-standing tent unless you know you'll be camping in a site with perfectly positioned trees.

Tents also come with a variety of window and door coverings. Netting is important for most campers because it helps keep insects outside the tent at night. Netting comes in two basic mesh sizes; mosquito netting will keep out the big bugs and no-see-um netting will keep out the little ones. We recommend no-see-um netting and believe that all tent openings should provide *both* nylon and netting covers. The openings should also use good zippers. We prefer heavy-duty nylon zips because they are relatively easy to repair and maintain. Metal zippers work well, too; snaps and tie closures don't.

For most uses, the design and shape of a tent is as much an aesthetic as a practical decision. Cost, size, and ease of setup can then be determining factors in selecting your tent. If you intend to try canoeing or backpacking, you'll generally want to go with a well-designed, lightweight (i.e., under 10 pounds), two- or four-person A-frame or dome. If you expect to be camping in severe winds or in the snow, you'll want to go with a dome. Cabin and umbrella tents, which come in sizes big enough for families and small armies, are so heavy and bulky that they are only useful for car camping, and we don't often recommend them. For groups of more than four, we usually recommend using two tents. And we don't generally recommend groups of more than eight.

For general use, we prefer a self-standing, two-person A-frame tent, like the Eureka Timberline™, or a modified A, like the Diamond Brand Mountain Spirit™, because they're relatively roomy and inexpensive. For real four season and backcountry camping, the Diamond Brand Mountain Creek™ is good, and the Moss Olympic™ (actually, our favorite) is great.

Sleeping Pads

If you are at all like us, you hate sleeping on cold, bare rocks. Our advice is not to. If you don't have a cot or motor home with you, a sleeping pad can help level out your bed spot and make for a much more comfortable rest. Four basic kinds of pads are commonly available: air mattresses, open-cell foam, closed-cell foam, and what we call, for lack of a better name, Therm-a-Rest type pads.

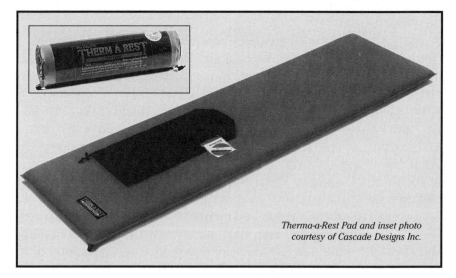

*Therma-a-Rest Pad and inset photo
courtesy of Cascade Designs Inc.*

Air mattresses tend to be very comfortable and are often quite inexpensive (99 cents and up). They also tend to get holes if you look at them cross-eyed. They are impossible to use on rough ground outside a tent because they puncture too easily, they're so slippery you have to tape them to your sleeping bag, and you have to inflate them every time you want to use them. They are simply much more work than they're worth. We don't like air mattresses, but you probably already noticed that.

Open-cell foam pads are as comfortable as air mattresses and just about as worthless for camping. They absorb water easily, do not insulate well, and if they're thick enough to be comfortable (4 to 6 inches), are bulky. Closed-cell pads, in contrast, don't absorb water, insulate well, and are more durable than most open-cell foam pads, or any other type of pad. Closed-cell foam pads come in a variety of thicknesses under a range of brand names. You can get a three-quarter-inch-thick pad (which is thick enough to be somewhat softer than the futon Curt and his cats sleep on at home) at a fabric store for just a few dollars, and it should work great for years with no maintenance or inflating. Specialty stores sell closed-cell foam pads for $10 to $20.

Therm-a-Rest type pads are really just a very thin piece of open-cell foam sealed inside a coated nylon bag. They are very comfortable, insulate exceptionally well, and, because they are sealed and waterproof, don't absorb water and don't need to be bulky. In fact, self-inflating pads really are nylon "air mattresses." The sealed nylon, though, is more durable than most plastics; and the foam inside expands by itself when you open the air valve, so you don't have to blow them up. They combine all the advantages of the other types of pad with almost none of the disadvantages.

The only disadvantages to using Therm-a-Rest™ pads are that they can leak—though good coated nylon is durable, hard to puncture, and fairly easy to patch—and they tend to be more expensive ($35 and up) than the other alternatives. They are also slippery, so if you buy one, consider getting some Slip Stop™ spray, too. Not surprisingly, Therm-a-Rest™ pads are the most readily available self-inflating pads; as far as we know, they are far and away the most comfortable camping pads on the market.

Pads come in full, about 72 inches, and less-than-full lengths. Full-length pads are the most comfortable, but shorter campers can easily get by with the three-quarter-length ones. Half-length

(torso) pads are uncommon and are really only for rugged individuals into ultra-light gear and massive discomfort or children who
are young enough and short enough to believe that 36 inches is
full length.

Sleeping Bags

Sleeping bags seem to vary more than almost any other type of
equipment in their size, material, insulation, shape, and construction. Don't let that intimidate you, though, because no matter how
much they vary or how complicated they are, all of them are
intended to serve a single purpose. Sleeping bags are made to
retain the heat your body generates while you sleep.

Because most people like to be comfortable at night—sleep can
be difficult if you're not—a good sleeping bag is very important.
The best way to find a good bag is to rent and test a number of different models and then to buy the one that works best. To shop for
a good bag, though, you do need to know a few things about them.

Comfort ratings are measures of the bag's insulating ability.
They represent the lowest temperature at which the bag is intended to be comfortable. These ratings are set by the manufacturers,
though, and are only a rough measure of the bag's ability to retain
heat. Because everyone has a different basal metabolism and pro-
duces different amounts of heat when they sleep, a bag rated to
30° Fahrenheit might serve some people well in 25° F weather, but
might not keep others warm at 50° F. What we're getting at here is
that you can't judge a bag by its rating. You should try a few different bags (many outdoor stores rent them out) before buying
one. You may want two or three for use under different conditions.

Bags come in three basic shapes: rectangles, modified rectangles, and mummies. The rectangular bag is the roomiest and will
generally unzip all the way around, so you can open it up and use
it as a blanket if you want or zip it together with another bag (top
to bottom). The biggest drawback to these bags, though, is also
their advantage—they have lots of room. In warm weather room is
great, but when it gets colder, extra space inside a bag is just
more space for your body to heat. Rectangular bags are not good
for cold-weather camping.

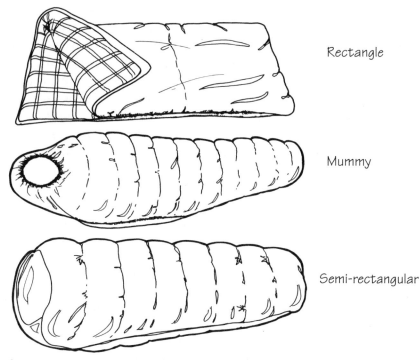

Rectangle

Mummy

Semi-rectangular

Semi-rectangular bags are wide open at the top, but taper off a bit toward the bottom—just like most people—so there's less extra space inside them. These bags often have a drawstring sewn in at the top, so you can close off the bag when it gets cold outside. Like rectangular bags, they usually have a full zipper and open up into blanket form or easily zip together with another identical bag; but unlike the rectangular bags, they don't have a lot of extra room. Consequently, semi-rectangular bags tend to be, ounce for ounce, somewhat warmer than their roomier counterparts.

Mummy bags conform, more or less, to the shape of the human body. They have a hood for your head, a wide top for your shoulders, and a narrow bottom for your feet. Mummies come with drawstrings, so you can seal yourself inside them, like a caterpillar in its cocoon. They generally use only three-quarter-length side zippers (to minimize heat loss), so you can zip two together only if one has a right-side and the other a left-side zipper. Mummy bags have the least extra room and extra material, so they pack more compactly than the other shapes, and, ounce for ounce, tend to be the warmest sleeping bag design on the market.

Bags also come with a number of insulations. Down, feathers, synthetics, cotton, and shredded newspaper (really) are all readily available. Down and a number of the synthetic insulators are worth considering, but feather bags, paper bags, and anything with cotton are not good for camping as these materials are exceptionally poor insulators under normal camping conditions— wet and cold.

Down provides, ounce for ounce, more "loft" (the thickness of the insulating layer) than any other material. Because loft, more than any other factor, determines the insulating value of a sleeping bag, down bags tend to be the warmest. Down is also highly compressible, so down bags pack very nicely. Down bags also tend to be lightweight; because down insulates so well you generally need less down than anything else to keep you warm. On the down side (please, pardon that pun), down absorbs moisture easily, it does not insulate well when it's wet, and it takes a long time to dry. Down is also relatively expensive.

The standard "fill" for down is about 550 cubic inches/ounce. If down is rated lower (that is, if it takes up less space when not compressed), be wary of it. You should also make sure any down you buy is down, and not just feathers. A good dictionary can explain the difference between the two. You should also get goose down, rather than duck down, because the former insulates better.

A number of the synthetic insulators work well when wet, absorb very little moisture, dry quickly, and are somewhat less expensive than down. The only real drawback with synthetics is that most of them are less compressible than down, and are less easily compressed, so they're harder to pack in small spaces. Synthetics don't provide as much insulation per ounce as down, either, so you generally need a heavier bag. On the other hand, synthetics will keep you warm even if they're wet, and down won't.

Thinsulate Lite Loft™ is one of the newest synthetic materials, and is, in some respects, the best synthetic on the market. It is almost as warm and compactible as down. Quallofil™ is one of our other favorites, and PolarGuard™ is really good too. Hollofil™ and a number of other synthetic insulations also work well. Each insulation offers its own advantages. When shopping, consider the life expectancy of the material, its loft and compressibility, and its insulating ability (warmth-to-weight ratio) both when wet and when dry.

The better bags will not be "sewn-through." Any time you sew through the insulating layer, you create a nice place for heat to escape the bag. Look for a bag with offset quilting, shingling or diagonal layering, or baffled construction. Any zippers should be covered by a hefty draft tube, a tube of insulation that prevents cold air from blowing in through the zipper, and the zippers themselves should be high-quality nylon and stiffened. All the material used in the bag should also be able to breathe (i.e., water permeable) or you might end up sleeping in a puddle of the water your body gives off through evaporation and respiration.

Good sleeping bags cost from $80 to $400, depending on the style, construction, and insulating material. Kids' bags are a little less. Don't settle for a $15 bag made for indoor use, or you will quickly learn to hate sleeping outdoors. We've both been happy with bags made by Sierra Designs, North Face, REI, and EMS. A number of other companies, including Kelty and Coleman (their Peak 1™ line), also make high-quality sleeping bags.

Packs

If you want to carry your camping equipment somewhere without making a bunch of trips back and forth, you'll need some sort of a pack. There's no reason to go out and buy an expensive backpack unless you're planning on backpacking, but a good day pack really is a must for people who plan to go hiking away from their base camp and equipment.

There are three basic types of packs: bags (which aren't really packs but do hold things), rucksacks, and frame packs. For car camping, any sort of bag will do for most of your equipment (even grocery bags will work ... but not well). If you're backpacking, a frame pack is a must, and for everything else, rucksacks work great.

A basic rucksack is really nothing more than a small bag with shoulder straps. For descriptive reasons we include in the category "rucksacks" all day packs, Duluth packs (large packs used almost exclusively for canoeing), and anything else that isn't a true frame pack. Many people use fanny-packs instead of small rucksacks for day hikes, but fanny-packs won't hold anything as large as a stove and coffee pot, so we suggest you consider adding a rucksack to your inventory of goods. A decent rucksack/day pack will usually cost upwards of $25.

Rucksack

Day packs come in a wide variety of shapes and sizes. We recommend that you get one about the same length as your back (measured along the spine from about the hips to the top of the shoulder). You will probably find that the little book bags many stores sell as day packs are too small to hold more than a sweater and are really uncomfortable. (They are cheap, though, and make good packs for kids.) You'll probably have to shop the specialty stores (or a good sports department at a general merchandiser) to find a good day pack—that is, one that is comfortable, has room for extra clothes, rain gear, a first-aid kit, a water bottle, and a few other small items, and doesn't cost too much.

Frame packs come with internal or external frames. External frames generally hold more weight and are great for use on trails and such. Internal frame packs are for use off trail in the woods or mountains; they hug your body so you can scramble or climb more easily. External frame packs generally cost $50 and up; internal frame packs of comparable quality cost about twice as much. These packs are described in more detail in Chapter 8.

Camp Trails makes a good, reasonably priced line of packs, including day packs and both internal and external frame packs. Kelty, Madden, Mountainsmith, REI, and EMS all make first-rate packs, too.

Luxury Items

A small hammock ($10 and up), a good book (free if you use the library), a small chair (canoe seats work great and are available from $12 to $60), and the proper wine with dinner (price depends on the wine) can all serve to make your trip a better one. If weight isn't a problem, a full-length lawn chair is a nice thing to have. Consider bringing such things if you have room in the car or canoe and can safely decant the wine into a plastic bottle or wine-skin.

If you don't care for these luxuries, at least consider a small sit pad (or sit-upon, if you grew up with the scouts). A small piece of closed-cell foam padding can make even the roughest wood bench a reasonably comfortable place to rest your weary bones.

Essential Personal Equipment

Map & Compass

Many parks and campgrounds provide visitors with reasonable maps showing all the area's roads and marked trails. If you have one and you won't be hiking off the trails or roads, you probably don't need anything better to help you navigate. If you need more details than the handouts provide, though, you'll have to go shopping for a map. When you do, consider three things: the map's accuracy, its orientation, and the amount of detail you'll need.

A map's accuracy is a function of its age, try to avoid historic maps, and the amount of work that went into producing it, so also avoid maps that look as if they were drawn up in a hurry. Reputable dealers will usually sell you reputable maps that are good enough to take you anywhere (assuming you know how to use a map). Anything that you can get for free will probably only be accurate enough for hiking on marked, paved trails.

A map's orientation is, more or less, the direction represented at the top of the page. Most maps are oriented to true north; that is, on most maps true north is up. It's important to know if your map is like most of the others, so make sure you can clearly see the orientation on any map you buy.

The amount of detail on your map is usually a function of two different things: the map type and its scale. Maps come in two basic types: topographical and non-topographical. (If you are a cartographer, please forgive us for our nontechnical language and marginally correct categorizations.) Topographical maps use *contour lines* to show the shape and location of the land features in the mapped area. This gives you much better and more useful information than you'll get from non-topographical maps. A *topo* is almost always a must if you'll be hiking off trails.

A map scale is the ratio between distance on the map and distance in the real world. On a 1:63,360 map, for example, one inch on the map is equal to one mile in the real world (5,280 feet/mile x 12 inches/foot = 63,360 inches/mile); and on a 1:250,000 map, one inch is equal to about four miles. Smaller ratios usually provide more details and better accuracy.

Some of the best maps available in and of the United States are produced by the USGS (United States Geological Survey, National Mapping Division). They have a detailed series which has 15 minutes of longitude per map and a very detailed series with 7.5 minutes—either of which can help you get from here to there.

You can get a free index of the USGS maps (indexed by state) by writing to the USGS Map Sales Office at Box 25286, Denver, CO 80225, for maps of the lower 48 states or USGS Map Sales, Alaska, 101 12th Avenue, Box 12, Fairbanks, AK 99701, for maps of Alaska. Similar services are provided in Canada through the Canada Map Office, 130 Bentley Ave., Nepean, Ontario K2E 6T9.

You can order your maps by mail if you know the map name, state or province, and series/scale—or you can buy them in person from a U.S. Geological Survey or Canada Map Office. You should be able to get the address of the one you need by calling the number listed in your phone book under Government Information. In the U.S., many states also have State Geological Survey Offices (Minneapolis, for example, has one for Minnesota) where you can get the same or very similar maps; the Ministry of Natural Resources provides that service in Canada. If you deal with the USGS or an affiliated state office, you might also consider asking for their guide to map symbols.

USGS or comparable quality maps of popular areas are usually available in the outdoor equipment stores as well, and a number of cities have commercial stores that specialize in selling maps. A store that stocks maps will probably be a lot faster than writing to the USGS (it is, after all, a government office; please allow six to eight weeks for delivery), but will probably cost you a bit more.

A good basic compass, to use in conjunction with whatever map you have, is useful even if you are staying on the marked trails. You never know when you'll need to know which direction is north, and you can't tell for sure without a compass. You can get a simple and reliable one for about $6 and up. All good general-use navigational compasses have three parts: a base plate with a direction-of-travel arrow; a housing marked in 1-, 2-, or 5-degree increments with a directional arrow printed on it; and a

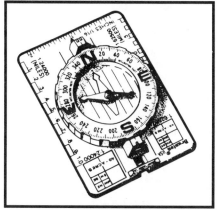

floating, magnetic directional arrow that is always supposed to point toward magnetic north.

Brunton, Silva, and Suunto all make good compasses, and the Boy and Girl Scouts of America (and a number of similar organizations) sell workable ones, too. A Silva Starter™ is one of the most basic "quality" compasses available. A Brunton Basic Map Compass, our current favorite, offers more advanced features like an adjustable declination

Compass illustration courtesy of Brunton/Lakota Outdoor Products

setting (discussed in Chapter 6) at a beginner's price.

First-Aid Kit

A first-aid kit is a really important piece of equipment. In fact, it's vital, and we always keep one handy when we're camping. It never hurts to be careful.

We've listed the contents of our basic personal first-aid kits. Since you aren't us, your kit will likely be a bit different because the kit has to meet your needs, not ours. You might, for example, want to add a home tooth extraction kit.

Whatever you decide, make sure you, and no one in your group, is allergic to anything you carry in your first-aid kit and avoid carrying any strong medicines that might make an emergency situation worse than it already is.

Basic First-Aid Equipment for Overnight Camping

anti-inflammatory (aspirin or ibuprofen)
analgesic (acetaminophen)
antacid
adhesive bandage strips (various shapes & sizes for minor cuts & scrapes)
moleskin or mole foam (for blisters)
antihistamine (for minor allergic reactions)
tweezers (for slivers)
roller gauze (2 @ 2" x 5 yards)
safety pins (several)
sterile gauze pads (at least 4 @ 4" x 4")
sanitary napkin (as bulk dressing for severe bleeding)
cloth tape (2" wide x 30')

triangle bandage
elastic bandages (2" ankle wrap & 4" knee wrap)
thermometer
2 quarters for phone calls & list of emergency numbers
anti-bacterial soap
calamine lotion
oval eye-pad
anti-fungal ointment
anti-bacterial ointment
personal medications
extra map & compass (for emergency use)

If you take a course in first aid, you'll be prepared to develop a kit that meets your specific needs, and you'll also make sure you know how to properly use everything you carry. We, of course, recommend such a course.

Candle Lanterns and Other Important Items

We generally don't use fires for anything, and when we do use a fire (in non-emergency situations), we put it out as soon as we're done with it. This makes it difficult to sit around the fire in the evening to talk or sing or sip tea. Since we do like to sit around, and a flame makes a good focal point, we almost always carry a candle lantern. These small, inexpensive ($12 and up), generally wind-proof candle holders work well at the center of a group gathering in the woods. Ours also provide enough light to read by if needed, and, unlike flashlights, they never need new batteries. They do, however, require extra candles at about 60 cents each and up. In hard times, a

one- or two-quart plastic bag with about 3" of dirt in the bottom and a small candle in the middle will serve in place of a candle lantern.

If you are camping out away from you car or plan to take day trips away from it, it is a good idea to carry some form of emergency shelter—a reflective rescue blanket, a heavy plastic bag, or a nylon tube tent will work well. It is also important to carry some emergency food. Some powdered soup, a bag of mixed nuts, a few hard candies, and whatever else you want to carry as emergency rations can make you more comfortable should you get lost or injured away from a source of immediate rescue. An extra candle, matches, and a cup can also be included in this emergency supplies' category. We always carry extra food and usually have a stove, pot, cup, spoon, matches, lighter, extra clothes, and parachute cord in our day packs, so we don't carry any formal emergency kit. Specialty stores do sell small emergency kits for $15 and up.

A repair kit is very important because something always needs fixing. Ours are composed of about three feet of light wire, some heavy thread, a needle, safety pins, and a role of duct tape. Yours should be similar, but might include such things as small tools (for stove or fishing-reel repair), buttons, stove parts, a spare compass, flashlight bulbs and batteries, a sewing kit, nylon patching tape, and other useful items. We don't carry too much because we both honestly believe that duct tape will fix anything that really needs fixing. Dan actually goes even further and contends that "life would be impossible without duct tape."

Toiletries

The importance of toilet paper should not need explaining, so we won't explain it. We will suggest, however, that you use plain white toilet paper (free of dyes or perfumes) made from recycled paper to minimize impacts on your body and the environment.

A trowel is necessary if you don't have plumbing facilities in your tent (which is usually the case) or trailer and such facilities aren't provided by the camping area managers. You'll use a trowel to dig a sump hole for cooking wastes and to dig cat-holes (small latrine pits) when no latrine or toilet is provided. Both of these uses are discussed in more detail in Chapter 6. We recommend a metal-handled trowel—they weigh more and cost more than the plastic ones, but break less easily.

Basic toilet articles are necessary because some hygiene is important even away from the city. We always like to brush our teeth, for example; and if the park provides a sink or shower facility, we like to wash with a mild biodegradable soap. If no washing facilities are provided, we often leave the soap at home (more on that in Chapter 6 under *Soap*). If you insist on showers even in the absence of shower facilities, you can always buy a Solar Shower™, a dark sun-absorbing water bladder, or something similar and carry it in your pack.

Tampons or sanitary napkins are an important consideration for women. A change in routine can affect your menstrual cycle, so it is a good idea to be careful and carry a supply even if you don't expect to need them.

Knives

A small pocket knife will come in handy when you are cooking and eating, when you're trying to fix things, and when you feel compelled to perform an emergency appendectomy on your neighbor. We prefer a single locking blade and refuse to carry a knife, other than a fish-filleting knife, with a blade longer than three inches. Anything bigger is just a waste of metal and a potential serious accident. Good knives, like Lakota's and the genuine and original Swiss Army models, start at about $15.

Less Essential but Necessary Personal Equipment

We think everyone who is out camping should have a water bottle she or he can easily carry on day hikes or the like. A one-quart (or one-liter) plastic bottle is perfect. We especially like the Nalgene™ wide-mouthed bottle. Canteens work great, too, but tend to be a bit too bulky and heavy.

We also recommend that each individual take responsibility for his or her own eating utensils—a cup or mug, a bowl, and a spoon are essential; a plate, a fork, and a knife sometimes are handy, too.

Flashlights should be small so they don't wake up the entire park system when you flash them around at night. We think head lamps are the nicest style for camping because they let you see in the dark but leave your hands free for setting up the tent or turning the pages of your book. It is also a good idea to carry a spare bulb and extra batteries for whatever flashlight you carry.

Sunscreen helps prevents sunburn. Sunglasses protect your eyes. Use both. Ultraviolet (UV) radiation can damage your skin and might damage your eyes; rather than deal with the possible problems too much sun can cause, you should prevent them.

A whistle can help you keep the kids under control and, should you get lost, might help you get found. On the odd occasion that a black bear or a curious skunk wanders into your campsite, a whistle can also be used to scare the wildlife. We like heavy metal whistles like the ones coaches use, but most people carry cheap plastic ones because they're easier to find in the stores. Your whistle should have a string or clip on it so you can carry it easily all the time.

A lot of experienced people consider pillows an unnecessary luxury on camping trips. We know better, and we often carry our nice comfy down and feather pillows with us when we camp. You can buy special "camp pillows," made from the same type of materials you find in sleeping bags, in the specialty stores, but unless weight and size are a major issue, you can get by with a bed pillow from home. We do, however, recommend a plastic pillow case.

A Final Note on Equipment

If you are camping out in a trailer or motor home, or are planning on living out of your car, most of this equipment isn't really necessary. Sheets and a blanket serve the same purpose as a sleeping bag, a lawn chair replaces a hammock, and a cot can replace a foam pad.

If you have a sense of adventure, though, and think you might like to try stepping beyond the confines of a trailer park, consider the equipment we've discussed here. It is suitable for beginners and is usable in a wide range of camping activities.

Chapter 4

You'd Better Shop Around Some More
Camping Clothes

Clothing is actually a part of your camping "equipment," but we are confident that, while you might wear your camping clothes in town, you won't use your Optimus stove anywhere off the trail. That makes clothes *special*, and since the chapter on equipment was getting way too long, we rationalized that this specialness merits clothes a chapter of their own.

One of our less reputable associates suggested that we should include a chapter on nude camping in this book, but unfortunately or not, we know nothing of substance about the subject. Neither of us camps in clothing-optional environments because we like to have clothes to protect us from scrapes, insect bites, sunburn, and the numerous other little hazards that congregate in the outdoors. In addition, clothes, when used correctly, help insulate against heat loss from convection, conduction, and to some degree, evaporation. Consequently, we feel they are a rather important part of a positive camping experience.

We almost always camp in places that require us to carry all of our food, equipment, and clothes with us at one time, in a canoe or a backpack. Since we like to eat a lot and need to carry the right equipment, we don't like to carry too many clothes. We figure that since we only need to wear one set of clothes at a time and we don't mind a little dirt, we only need to carry a maximum of two sets of clothing each on a trip.

The list provided below is all the clothes we take with us on camping trips of almost any length during the spring and fall. During the summer, we leave a few of the warmer pieces at home, and during the winter, we carry a few really specialized pieces.

We've broken this list into layers because it is important for you to layer your clothes when you're camping. With three or four layers of lightweight clothes (as opposed to a single heavy layer) you can regulate your body temperature quite easily. If you're hot, remove a layer; if you're cold, add one. It is a good idea to add and subtract layers before you get *too* hot or *too* cold. If you never sweat, you stay dryer, more comfortable, and cleaner; and if you never get cold, you'll be a much happier camper.

Minimum Clothing List for Flatland Campers Spring, Summer, or Fall Camping

Head Wear
  hat with brim
  wool stocking cap

First Layer
  2 pair underwear (nylon, wool,
    polyester, or poly/cotton)
  2 T-shirts (nylon, polyester, or
    poly/cotton blend)
  long underwear tops &
    bottoms (wool or polypropylene)
  3 or 4 pairs wool socks
  wool gloves

Second Layer
  1 pair shorts (polyester or canvas)
  1 pair long wool or
    fleece pants

(Second Layer cont.)
  1 long-sleeved wool or
    fleece shirt
  1 lightweight down vest or
    second wool shirt.
  1 pair sneakers or moccasins
  1 pair of light or medium boots
    (or second pair of sneakers)

Last Layer
  raincoat
  rain pants
  windbreaker
  wind pants

Bandanas
  3–12 in various colors

Fashion in the Out-of-Doors

Good clothes for camping are quite easy to find at specialized outdoor stores, and you'll probably need to go to one of those places if you want to get really trendy clothes. With the exception of a few specialized pieces, though, clothes suitable for camping tend to be just as available, and much less expensive, at your local thrift shop. If you don't have a thrift shop handy, you can also check out your nearest department store, or better yet, the nearest discount store.

As a general rule, function should take precedence over form in camping clothes—style is really nice in the city, but in the woods, practicality is much more important. Forsaking fashion can also save you a lot of money as you generally pay a premium for up-to-date stylishness. Be sure not to skimp too much, though. Woods' wardrobes can (and should!) follow some fashion rules of their own.

Unfortunately, fashion rules, in the woods as everywhere else, are subject to whims. In our opinion, for example, "camo" prints are best left to active hunters, splat-ball players, and kids who want to pretend they're veterans. Other rules are, fortunately, more consistent. Bright colors, for example, are an absolute no-no—except during hunting season.

Current trends suggest that huge pockets are "in," while slashed knees are "out." Plaid shirts are almost a must, while paisley pants are an anathema. Keep this in mind when you are planning your camping attire—the fashion police have been known to issue citations even in the most remote wilds.

You should also keep in mind that it really does matter what fabric you wear. That's why we're offering information about some of the most common fabrics used in camp clothing.

Natural Fibers

Cotton is a wonderful fiber. In sheltered areas (i.e., those in which you can stay dry and out of the wind), it is great for camping. Denim jeans are inexpensive, durable, and comfortable; so are cotton T-shirts, underwear, and socks. Unfortunately, cotton wicks moisture very well and very quickly, which means that if you get the cuffs on your jeans wet, you will soon be wet from the waist down. This wouldn't be a real problem except for the fact that cotton does not insulate at all when it is wet. In fact, wet cotton will keep you colder than nothing at all. It's a darn shame that sheltered campsites are so rarely available; but because they are so rare, we generally recommend that all of your cotton remain at home when you go camping away from your car or some other heated shelter. Or at least most of it.

Canvas is a good camping material, for shoes and maybe for a tarp or tent. Canvas clothes are bulky and generally should only be worn by hard-core sailors.

Poplin (usually corded cotton; sometimes wool, rayon, or silk) and chino (twilled cotton) share the characteristics of the materials from which they are made. If you are going to ignore us and wear your comfy cotton clothes, at least be sure they are made from one of these fabrics. Poplin and chino tend to be more water repellent and abrasion resistant than other cotton fabrics. They are also much more cool (with it? hip?) ... especially in khaki.

Wool is another wonderful all-natural fiber. Unlike cotton, though, wool and the woods really seem to go together. Wool wicks moisture and dries fairly slowly; but it insulates really well when wet, is very durable, and a lot of us experienced campers think it defines the word "comfortable." If you do buy wool, make sure it's virgin, as opposed to reprocessed, and processed as little as possible so it retains its natural lanolin—an oil that helps make it water repellent.

Wool is great for underwear, socks, slippers, hats, mittens, gloves, shirts, pants, blankets, sweaters, and jackets. In some countries it's used to build shelters. It can be spun and woven, knitted, felted, or left, fleecily, on the tanned hide of the sheep that bore it. It is a wonderful fiber.

For woolen underclothes, fine weaves are generally more comfortable than rough ones, but even finely woven wool might chaff in sensitive spots; because of that, and because not everyone likes the warm scratchy feeling of wool next to the skin, you might want to consider some of the synthetics discussed below for first-layer clothes, or use cotton in warm weather. It is hard to beat wool knits, though, for socks, hats, and sweaters; and woven wool makes great pants and wonderfully warm shirts that feel right at home in the woods. Ragg-wool socks, which are knit from thick wool yarn, were almost certainly invented in heaven.

Rayon is sort of a natural fiber (it's made from processed wood cellulose), so we'll add it to the list here. Rayon is not especially durable and it's not a good insulator, but it is comfortable when the weather is hot and humid. That may be why the best Hawaiian print shirts are made from rayon. You might want a Hawaiian shirt for any formal dinners you have to attend when you're camping. They don't weigh much and hardly take up any space at all in a pack, so consider taking one whenever, and wherever, you go.

Silk has always been one of our favorite natural fibers. It is comfortable as all-get-out and makes some of the warmest long johns imaginable. We also happen to like wearing silk T-shirts in any weather, in spite of the mobs of admirers they attract. The only drawbacks here are cost and durability for outerwear; the first is too high and the latter too low.

Leather is a great natural fiber, but only for boots, mittens, and gloves. Leather clothes absorb water like cotton, and usually shrink and get real stiff when they dry. Unless you really want to try walking like John Wayne did in his cowboy days (we think that more than his lips were chapped!), don't wear leather clothes when you're camping.

Down is a natural fiber, and it is sometimes used to insulate clothes. Even though down is usually too warm for summer use, almost nothing is as slick as a down vest over a red-and-gray plaid wool shirt; the combination will make you look like an experienced woodsperson. Fashion-conscious campers should check the sleeping bag section for more information about down.

Synthetic Fibers

Nylon is probably the most common synthetic fabric you'll encounter when shopping for camping clothes and equipment. It is relatively inexpensive, durable, suited to a wide range of uses, and can be wind and/or waterproof. You can buy nylon versions of almost any article of clothing you'd consider wearing, but experienced campers (the ones we know, at least) generally use it only in their outer layers of clothing. You'll find more about nylon in the previous chapter in the sections on tents and tarps.

Polyester is another great synthetic fiber. It's hard to go wrong with it when you're camping—unless you buy one of those awful double-knits left over from the early seventies or (thinking about it makes us shudder) a leisure suit. Polyester is commonly used for underclothes, pants, shirts, and shorts, alone or in concert with cotton. The poly/cotton blends, at least 60 percent polyester and no more than 40 percent cotton, make very useful summer camping clothes, especially T-shirts. Polyester is useful because it can be made to imitate the look and feel of cotton, but it is less absorbent and a better insulator. It's also used to make some piles, buntings, and fleeces.

Pile, fleece, and bunting are, more or less, different names for what can be loosely called "synthetic wools." These materials are warm, lightweight, and don't hold moisture well. While wool can hold up to 40 percent of its weight in water, most fleeces hold only 5 percent or less of their weights in water, so they dry very quickly. We also think that the buntings and similar fabrics are really, really comfortable. A whole lot of people share this last opinion—unlike many of our others. These fabrics do tend to be bulkier than wool, however, so they don't pack too compactly, and they don't break the wind at all, while tightly woven wool can. If you buy bunting, you also need a windbreaker—actually, you need a windbreaker whether you buy bunting or not.

Polypropylene is one of the synthetics commonly used in less expensive camping clothes. It wicks moisture (absorbs and transports it) away from your body, so the moisture can easily evaporate. It dries quickly and insulates well. A wide range of comparable polyester synthetics are also available and are used in underwear, shirts, pants, hats, gloves, socks, and just about everywhere else. The only problem we've ever had with polypropylene is its smell—actually our smell—which is hard to wash completely out of the clothes (without a special soap) once they've been used. Such is life! The newer wicking synthetics, like Patagonia's Capilene™, DuPont's Thermax™, and REI's MTS™, don't share this problem, but they tend to be a little more expensive than the older polypropylene.

A whole bunch of other synthetics are used effectively in camping clothes, but we're not going to discuss them here as nearly all of them share some combination of the properties we've already mentioned. Anyway, most of them are just variations on nylon or polyester.

It is really impossible to say which fabrics are "best"—even for people as opinionated as we are—because what is best for one person in a particular situation is not always good for another. Fortunately, for summer camping it's hard to go wrong with almost any well-made clothing. After a while, once you've tried a few different materials, you can decide for yourself which best suits your needs. If you are shopping for camping clothes, some key points to consider are the wet and dry insulating properties of the material used, its wind and water resistance, its durability, its weight (and compressibility if you're into backpacking), and its price in relation to comparable fibers.

In our discussion of fabrics, we worked from the theory that it can get cold enough to matter at any time of the year, so we focused on materials that will keep you warm when the sun fails to do so. In reality, sometimes it does stay warm all of the time.

We tend to push synthetics because they work so well when the weather turns cooler, but if you can reasonably expect very warm weather and you aren't worried about some extra weight, you might possibly consider carrying a few cotton items. Chinos, a cotton shirt, and some cotton sweat socks can be comfortable when it's hot out, as can loose-fitting poly/cotton blends and rayon. That said, each item of clothing bears some discussion.

Head Wear

A cotton or wool crusher, a baseball cap, a sombrero, or any similar hat with a brim is important. It can help keep you dry in light rains, it keeps the sun off your head and out of your eyes, and it covers up messy hair. We know a lot of people who like to use a hat to carry all the pins and buttons from the parks they've visited, and hats are a good place for those. We don't think they're a good place for fishing lures, though. Hooks in the eye are a serious bummer. Anti-sun hats (the brimmed ones) should be vented or made from material that can breathe, and it's nice if they're water repellent. Light colors are coolest because they reflect sunlight, but dark colors on the underside of the brim absorb light and make seeing easier.

A wool stocking cap might seem a bit extreme when its 90° F outside, but we carry one anyway. Even in the summer. When it's wet out, or cools off unexpectedly, a ragg-wool hat can really help you keep warm. We both carry one in our sleeping bag stuff sack,

Clothing Materials – Summary Table of Our Opinions

Material	Insulation when dry	Water Absorption	Drying Time	Insulation when wet	Wind Resistance	Water Repellancy	Durability	Weight Overall	Rating	Best Uses
Cotton	moderate	very high	slow to very slow	non-existent	generally low, moderate for tight weaves	very low	depending on weave or knit	medium to heavy	poor	Underwear (cool & warm weather), socks, occasional T-shirts or jeans (warm weather only)
Canvas	not relevant (we don't recommend canvas clothes)	low to moderate (depending on how treated)	slow to very slow	not relevant (we don't recommend canvas clothes)	moderate	moderate to high depending on weight & treatment	high	very heavy	poor	shoes (sneakers) & possibly tarps
Poplin & Chino	moderate	moderate to high	very slow	moderate to low if wool, rayon, or silk; very low if cotton	low	low; so-so for chino	moderate	medium to heavy	so-so	warm-weather pants
Wool	high	high	very slow	high	low to moderate (depending on weave & lanolin content)	moderate to high (depending on weave & lanolin content)	high	medium to heavy	excellent	socks, pants, shirts, sweaters, hats, mittens, gloves, long johns
Rayon	low	high	fast	low	low	low	low	light	good	warm-weather shirts & Hawaiian prints
Silk	high	moderate	fast	high	low	low	moderate to low (for underwear & liners), very low (for outerwear)	light	very good	underwear (especially long johns), sock liners, glove liners, very comfortable T-shirts
Leather	moderate	high	very slow	moderate	high	moderate to high	high	heavy	very good	boots & shoes, work gloves, mittens & maybe hats
Nylon	moderate	generally low, depending on material	fast	moderate	moderate to very high	moderate to very high depending on coating	high	light	very good	tarps, tents, sleeping bags, rain gear, wind gear, packs, jackets, shoes/boots
Polyester	moderate	low	fast	moderate	low to moderate	moderate to high	high	light	excellent	alone or blended with cotton in underwear, pants, shirts, shorts, jackets, T-shirts
Pile, fleece & bunting	high	very low	fast	high	low (should be layered with a windbreaker)	moderate	high	light	excellent	cool & cold weather jackets, pants, hats, mittens, gloves

so we always know where it is. A good double-layer, knitted wool hat will be warmer than the less expensive polyester and acrylic ones we usually see on sale and is well worth the few extra dollars it will cost.

First Layer
Underclothes

Underwear is, well you know, sort of hard to talk about. We're not sure why, but it's supposed to be embarrassing to mention it. Putting such social conventions aside for a moment, we'd like to suggest that underwear is a good thing. Our moms always told us to wear clean underwear just in case we got in a car accident. That might not be a bad idea (though we're not sure it's a good one either), but we're not real worried about accidents here. We figure that you should wear clean undies as a matter of hygiene and to prevent chaffing.

When we're camping our preference is for polyester or nylon underwear because we pack light and both materials dry quickly after they're washed. It is possible to get by with only two pairs of underwear since you can wash and dry one pair while you're wearing the second—if you like this technique, you too might prefer nylon boxers or briefs. If you're camping from a car and don't need to carry all your gear on your back, bring along as many pairs of briefs (or whatever) as you like. If you plan on wearing wool pants at any time during your adventure, we think that bringing at least one pair of boxer shorts along, for men and women, is a good idea; the inside of your thighs will probably agree with us.

T-Shirts

For T-shirts we recommend spun polyester or a poly/cotton blend. Polyester doesn't rinse out as nicely as nylon, but it seems to be a whole lot more comfortable. You might want to carry at least one dark-colored shirt, to absorb sunlight and keep you warm, and one light-colored one, to reflect sunlight and keep you cool. If you camp the way we do, both shirts will be sort of a dirty brown by the end of the trip, but it's nice to try planning ahead anyway. Acid rock band logos on camping T-shirts are definitely out, for anyone over thirteen, so avoid them. Apart from that, just about any T-shirt will work.

Long Johns

Long underwear tops and bottoms make great pajamas for warm sleeping on cold nights. When worn under shorts, the bottoms can also serve to keep you warm on days that are too hot for long wool pants but too cold for just shorts. You can buy all sorts of long johns, but we recommend either silk or a synthetic material like Capilene™ because these materials are warm, dry easily, and wick moisture away from your body, which helps create a comfortably dry layer of warm air next to your skin. Wool is also an effective material for long underwear, but it tends to be more abrasive than the other materials. Cotton long johns really don't do much good once you sweat enough to get them moist (and if you're alive you will), so if you carry cotton long johns, don't wear them when you want to stay warm. If you're camping near your car, you might want to substitute a sweat suit for long underwear, at least in the summer. Sweats—poly/cotton blends, please—are very comfortable, reasonably warm, and far more stylish, in some circles, than a union suit. If things get too cold for sweats, you can always drive to the nearest motel.

Socks

Ragg-wool socks are wonderful, but in spite of their heavenly nature, they aren't your only sock option. Wearing synthetic or silk socks or liners is fine, and even cotton works well if you are camping near your car or an indoor shelter (or the weather stays real warm). Wool socks are the best, though, because they will help keep your feet comfortable even if they get wet. Neither of us find them to be too itchy, but if you do, wear them over a silk or synthetic liner.

When hiking, even for a day, you should consider wearing two pairs of socks. This helps keep your feet dry, and friction between the two layers of socks replaces much of the friction that would otherwise exist between your shoes and feet. If you wear two layers of socks (one light, one heavy), you're less likely to get blisters.

The third, and/or fourth, pair of stockings on the minimum list is for evening wear only. As soon as you're done hiking and playing, you should air out your feet and put on dry socks and shoes. Life is so much more pleasant with dry footwear that it's well worth the effort.

Gloves

Wool gloves, like the stocking hat, are probably not necessary during the summer. But if it does get cold, they're a blessing. We often wear gloves when we're canoeing, too, to prevent blisters. The only drawback is that wet hands inside gloves tend to get very, very chapped. If we expect cold weather when we go camping, we take mittens (choppers with wool liners and leather covers) as well as our ragg-wool gloves. You might want to, too, as cold hands are almost as uncomfortable, in our little world at least, as wet feet or the wrong wine with dinner.

If you aren't used to working or cooking outside, you might also want to bring a pair of leather or cotton work gloves to protect your hands from briars, brambles, insects, and hot pots.

Second Layer

Shorts

Shorts are not usually our first choice in recommended leg wear for hiking in the woods. We've scraped up our legs too often to really believe in them, and long pants offer better protection against ticks, flies, and an assortment of other potential hazards. Hot weather, though, makes shorts something of a necessity for many people.

We recommend long shorts—maybe not long enough to reach your knees, but close—that have huge pockets. You might find it helpful to have a pair with pockets big enough for you to carry your lunch in them so you can eat easily while walking along the trail. Our hiking shorts are the only 100 percent cotton clothing we regularly take into the backcountry. Any shorts will work, though. We know a lot of people who wear those skimpy nylon running shorts, or even polyester, nylon, or cotton swimsuits or "jammers" when the weather is warm.

Swimwear

Our shorts double as swimsuits (on those rare occasions when we swim in an area that requires real swimwear), but you might want to add a real swimsuit to your clothing list. A note of caution. Do not wear the same swimsuit all the time because swimsuits tend to be great breeding grounds for bacteria. This creates problems for men and women, but especially for women. If you wear a suit, change it or clean it as often as you would underwear.

Long Sleeves and Legs

Long pants and a long-sleeved shirt are especially important for evening wear. You'd be surprised how cool even 75° F is when you're camping out. We love wool, so we usually recommend it, but fleece or bunting is almost as warm and, some say, even more comfortable. We also carry down vests with us most of the time in case the weather is colder than expected. They work wonders when it comes to insulating your body core and hardly take up any room at all in a pack.

Summer campers might want to substitute a chamois shirt for a wool one and to add some long chinos or other long pants to their minimum clothing list. Cotton shirts and pants tend to be comfortable and cool, as long as the weather is good, and they also have a long history of use as anti-insect wear. When the insects are particularly bad, long pants and a long-sleeved shirt provide better protection than any insect repellent we know of.

Shoes and Boots

We always take two pairs of shoes camping; one for daytime wear and one for evening wear. If we're backpacking with a heavy load we wear light boots, otherwise we almost always stick to sneakers or walking shoes.

Heavy boots are environmentally destructive. If you walk on loose soil or delicate vegetation in heavy boots, you are apt to take a large chunk of that environment away with you. The extra weight tied to your feet is also a common source of discomfort. So, if you don't need to wear boots, don't.

A lot of people recommend high-top boots because conventional wisdom says that the uppers provide extra ankle support. We're not convinced that this is always true. High tops do protect your ankles from abrasion, but in our experience, they're usually not high enough to prevent sprains. No boot, high or low, can substitute for careful walking, which is by far the best way to prevent ankle injuries. Low tops are what most people are used to, and what people are accustomed to wearing is generally most comfortable. Because comfort is important, don't feel obligated to go out and buy high-top boots or shoes.

The soles on your shoes are an important consideration. If you are going to be walking on rough surfaces—boulders and the like—a lugged or cleated sole (the kind Vibram™ makes) can prevent a lot of unnecessary slipping and sliding. On trails and smoother surfaces, any reasonably stiff, rough sole, like those on decent running shoes, should suffice to keep you moving in the direction you want to go. A stiff sole can also help prevent bruises on the soles of your feet. If you are going to carry any weight, other than your own, or are planning to walk more than you usually do, good arch support is also a must.

Last Layer

We didn't expend much space discussing clothing design or construction in the discussion of the first two layers because most people know how to look for well-made "street" clothes, and camping clothes aren't much different from normal everyday ones. The last layer, though, is generally more specialized, and the designs that are best for camping aren't the same as those used for town clothes.

Rainwear

An umbrella might suffice in the city, but if you want to enjoy camping, good rain gear is very important. We usually recommend that campers carry both a raincoat and matching rain pants. Such a fully waterproof suit will enable you to continue your outdoor activities, in relative comfort, through most normal rainstorms (lightning is a different story). Just wearing a raincoat, in contrast, will not keep you dry unless you crouch down low enough to make the jacket cover your legs as well as your torso and wait for the rain to go away.

We recall one trip (actually several trips) when we waited for the rain to go away for ten days. It never did! That's why we like rain suits.

Rain suit materials range from cheap plastic to coated nylon to Teflon (Gore-Tex™ and the like). Plastic is inexpensive, and nothing is as waterproof, in our opinion, as the old yellow rubberized plastic fisherpersons' jackets we used to have. For occasional use, plastic is functional. If you don't plan on subjecting your rain suit to any abrasion, awkward stretching, or any crashing through the woods (which, unfortunately, are outcomes of most of our camping activities), plastic is also durable enough. If you're on a tight budget, plastic rain gear might suffice.

Breathable rain suits are really impressive and are certainly worth considering. Materials like Gore-Tex™, REI Elements™, Helly-Tech™, and Air-Weave™ are made with microscopic pores that let water vapor (sweat and the like) out, but don't let big old rain drops in. These fabrics really do work; however, they generally cost a lot more than traditional non-breathing materials. Expedition-quality rain gear is usually made from breathable material nowadays, but such suits aren't really necessary on typical, short camping trips.

The rain gear material we usually recommend is urethane-coated nylon. Coated nylon is as waterproof as, and more durable than, almost anything else on the market, and it is usually reasonably priced, too.

Good nylon or breathable rain gear is usually hard to find except in outdoor specialty stores or catalogues. Plastic rain suits are sold almost everywhere you can buy a fishing lure.

Rain gear comes in a wide range of styles and shapes. Cagoules, ponchos, and jackets are the most common upper-body covers. Thigh-length jackets (we include anoraks in this category) are generally the most versatile rain covers. It is easy to walk in them, or paddle a canoe, or fish, or just sit around. Cagoule, long below-the-knee-length pullovers, are best for sitting in a boat, but they will work almost anywhere and are a good investment if you don't have rain pants. Ponchos, with all due respect to the Scouts, are essentially worthless. They blow around so much that they rarely keep you dry, and they are impossible to work in. Whatever style you decide on, remember that a hood is a must, as are pockets, storm flaps sewn in to cover any zippers, and, if your cover has sleeves, cuffs that close with snaps or Velcro™. Waist belts are nice to have on jackets (inside is better, but outside works) to keep the wind from blowing up your shirt. Seamless shoulders and "factory sealed" seams really help keep the rain out, too.

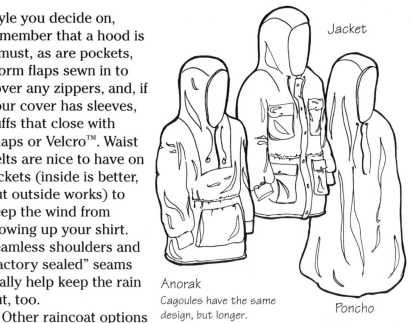

Jacket

Anorak
Cagoules have the same design, but longer.

Poncho

Other raincoat options include vents (front, back, and under the arms), liners made from material like Taslan™ that are intended to wick sweat away from your skin, powder skirts (strips of material connected to the inside of the coat that snap around your waist to keep rain from blowing under the coat) in place of belts, and all sorts of other gimmicky things. Curt's favorite raincoat (the coated nylon one) is actually an anorak designed for kayaking. It has Velcro™ closures on neoprene (the material used in wet suits) cuffs, a bunting liner in the collar, a polypropylene lined hood, pockets in front and on one sleeve, and vents under the sleeves. He loves every trendy inch of it, especially the vents, because they make it easier to adjust body temperature without losing the waterproof outer layer. Dan's favorite is a similar design, but it's made from Gore-Tex™.

Rain pants and chaps are the most common varieties of lower-body rain gear; to our knowledge, they're the only ones. Pants can be waist high or bib overall styles. Chaps, just like the old cowboy clothes, only cover the front of the camper's legs. Guess which design we prefer? If you guessed pants, you're right. Our rain pants are designed just like sweat pants, except they have snaps and elastic in the cuffs, and an inside pocket. You can get rain pants with full-length side zippers, drop seats, dozens of pockets, and secret decoder rings built in, but all you really need is something to keep your legs dry. Pants come in the same materials as jackets. Go with your instincts on this item.

Wind Gear

The best wind gear is made from lightweight nylon. If you carry a windbreaker and wind pants, you'll probably wear them quite often to prevent sunburn and to keep insects away from your delicate skin. Most people find that a windbreaker (jacket or anorak) or wind shirt is enough, and wear rain pants or long pants in lieu of wind pants. If you plan on spending a lot of time walking in (as opposed to on or near) cold water, you might consider wearing long underwear and wind pants. The combination is pretty warm and it dries in just a few minutes.

The Bandana

We know it may seem extreme to some of you, but we really think the bandana deserves a section all its own. We love bandanas. They serve equally well as handkerchiefs, head wear, towels, and pot holders. Two tied together at the corners can make a serviceable shirt, and a large one makes a decent diaper. We've worn bandana scarves and seen them used as flags, fans, sponges, pot scrubbers, pants, paper (for writing letters home), and packs. They can also be used as bulk dressings, to tie splints in place, and to make serviceable slings and wrist wraps. Always carry a few when you're camping, and be creative in using the dang things.

Optional Items

If you are planning on hiking a lot, you might want to invest in a set of gaiters. These handy little items of apparel are great for keeping loose gravel (and snow, too, if you ski at all) out of your boots or shoes. The bottom half of gaiters should be waterproofed and the top half shouldn't be. We like either Gore-Tex™ or coated nylon bottoms with 60/40, 60 percent nylon, 40 percent cotton, cloth tops.

Some of the women we know prefer sports or jogging bras over the more traditional models. The additional support provided by these items of clothing can help prevent uncomfortable chafing and bouncing during the strenuous activities that often accompany camping.

Down booties or fleece-lined camp slippers are really nice to have when the temperature drops. They are even warmer than ragg wool and can really help keep a smile on your face no matter how cold it gets.

Chapter 5

And Such Small Portions!
Food for the Camper

There is an old story, often told around the candle lantern at night, about a group of friends who were on an extended trip in the wilds. One, when designated cook by his companions, agreed to wield the ladle only as long as there were no complaints. Day after day he prepared meals for his friends, day after day he grew less fond of his role, and day after day he took less care in the preparation of the evening meal. No one else wanted to cook, so no one would complain. Finally, in a fit of desperation, the designated cook baked some moose scat into a casserole. During dinner that night there were moans and grimaces. There was a long awkward pause as the friends contemplated their plates, and finally one of the campers blurted out, "Man, this tastes like moose dung." After a moment of shocked silence he added briskly, "And such small portions, too!"

About Cooking in Camp
If you know how to cook in a kitchen, you should be able to cook just fine in camp. Remember, though, that camp stoves usually only run on *high* and on *very high*, that charcoal works just the same in a fire pit as it does in a grill, and that fires are as hot as gas stoves, but a lot less predictable. We think you need to plan foods that require a lot of heat when they're cooking.

If you don't know how to cook in a kitchen and want to eat more than cold cereal and bagels, bring along a friend who can cook. Pay bribes if you have to. Food is far too important to leave to chance or beginners.

As for lessons, well, we really don't believe it's possible for anyone to learn how to cook, in camp or anywhere else, from a single short section in a book. You'll have to learn to cook on your own or buy our sequel (*Over the Fire and Into Your Mouth*) when we write it.

What we can do, though, is to share what we know about nutrition as it applies to camping, throw a couple of traditional recipes your way, and give you a few pointers about what food goes well with a tent and sleeping bag.

Food Planning

Planning food begins with an understanding of who will be eating. As you will, presumably, be eating the food you take camping with you, plan for things you like. This conflicts directly with some of the more hard-boiled advice books we've seen, those that prescribe certain diets or menus. If you want to be happy, you've got to like what you're eating. So does everyone else you're camping with, so plan for them, too.

Be especially careful if anyone in your camping party has any food allergies—prepackaged and dried meals often have some surprising ingredients hidden inside, like milk solids in spaghetti sauce. Read the labels carefully!

What you eat when you're camping depends partly on what you like, but because "you are what you eat" (that is, what you eat affects how well your body functions), you should also consider what nutritional demands camping places on your body. Plan your diet accordingly.

If you're planning a vehicle-based trip and you really prefer to eat perishable foods, invest in a good cooler or ice chest ($20 and up). But even the best ice chest needs fresh ice every day or two, so we recommend that you leave the cooler at home and bring along foods that will keep for a few days, or weeks, without refrigeration.

Plan on eating often when you're camping. If you're hiking or doing anything else that's very active, food is much easier to carry in your stomach than in your pack; and when you're just sit-

68

ting around, eating can be a lot of fun. Cooking and eating are wonderful opportunities for social interaction that might otherwise be subordinated to individualized recreational plans.

Nutrition and Camping

To remain healthy, the "average" active adult camper needs to consume three to four quarts of water and about 2500 to 3500 calories each day, and up to about 5000 calories/day in the winter. This might seem like a lot to people who normally sit at a desk, but it really isn't. Camping involves physical activity and physical activity consumes energy. Humans produce energy only if they consume sufficient water and calories. A pair of simple formulas to remember are:

$$\text{water + calories = human metabolism = heat}$$
$$\text{and}$$
$$\text{heat = energy = work}$$

This means that you need to give what you are eating a bit of thought.

If you are planning a trip that requires you to actually carry your food, it is possible to pack all you need into about two pounds of (dried) food per person per day. This weight allotment does not include packaging (cans, bottles, etc.) or water.

As far as nutrition goes, if you know what to eat at home, you'll do just fine when you're camping by eating mostly the same things. Just plan on eating more of them. There are a few things related to nutrition that you might want to consider.

Plan on eating more starchy foods such as breads, grains, cereals, and fruit when you're camping than you do at home. They provide a good source of energy and aren't a bad source of roughage either. In fact, a high-carbo bagel is usually a better source of "quick" energy than a chocolate bar.

To make sure that you get enough protein, consider at least one meal a day that provides all eight of the amino acids that your body can't produce on its own. Meat, fish, poultry, and eggs are all sources of all of those amino acids; grains, seeds, dairy products, and legumes each provide some of them. The complementary protein chart shows which food groups or items can be combined to provide all eight of these essential amino acids if you're camping sans cooler and can't eat meat.

Complementary Proteins
(with selected examples)

Food groups in which selected items are complementary

Grains + Seeds
rice cakes with
sesame seeds

Milk Products & Legumes
milk in legume soup
cheese sauce & chick peas

Milk Products & Seeds
sesame and milk

Food groups in which foods are generally complementary

Grains & Milk Products
bread made with milk
cereal with milk
cheese sandwiches on wheat bread
macaroni and cheese
peanut butter and whole wheat bread

Grains + Legumes
lentil stew with rice
bean chili & rice or
wheat bread
corn tortillas & beans

Seeds + Legumes
sunflower seeds & peanuts
humus
roasted soy
nuts & seeds

Balanced Meals

A balanced meal is not necessarily one in which the appetizer and dessert are equally weighted, as nice as that might sound. Generally the "balance" in a balanced meal is between the various food groups, or between the nutritional contents of the meal and the nutritional needs of the eater.

The nutritional demands made by camping can generally be met quite easily by planning a varied diet that includes proteins (two servings/day), milk products (four servings/day), fruits or vegetables (four servings/day), grains or cereals (four servings/day), and lots of water. Because a lack of vitamin C can make you grumpy, or so some say, it is a good idea to carry some source of that vitamin, but it really isn't overly important to worry about most of the others. Some vitamins may be lacking in your camping diet because the food will be mostly dried, but as long as you get enough water and a sufficient number of calories from that diet, any minor shortages won't affect you much over the course of a few days.

Fluids

It is rather strange, but unfortunately true, that thirst is not a good indication of a need for fluids. You usually won't feel as thirsty as you ought to feel, so it is important to remember to drink often, even when you're not thirsty. You should drink three to four quarts of water, or other clear liquids, every day when you're out camping. If you're really active, it's necessary to drink even more than that. Don't forget. It's important. Really.

While we're on this subject, it is also important to note that, while adults and children don't usually have trouble with over-hydration, infants might. So, if you're taking your baby camping, be sure to check with your pediatrician about appropriate levels of fluid intake.

Camp Cooking

Where you cook is easy. In prepared campsites, we think it's a good idea to cook and eat at the picnic table. In other locales, it's probably best to cook and eat away from flammable items like tents and near a source of water; your water bottle or water bladder is fine. Stay off trails when you're eating and be sure to keep away from delicate or poisonous plants. We've both seen people carelessly sit in patches of poison ivy during lunch, and we love to imagine how uncomfortable that might make dinner.

How you cook is dependent on how many stoves you carry, the equipment in your trailer's kitchen, or your experience with charcoal or fires. We usually carry two stoves and always enjoy hot beverages, so we prefer cooking everything we can in a single pot. This is called, not surprisingly, one-pot cooking. Sometimes we take our time and cook more elaborate meals, but generally we stick to boiled soups, stews, and pastas.

If you insist on trying to cook on a fire—in spite of our sage advice—be prepared to eat (and if possible, enjoy) burned food, at least until you get the hang of cooking everything on high. If you plan to cook on charcoal, practice at home first.

Food Ideas & Suggestions

Fresh foods are good at home and even better when you're camping, so we don't recommend that you rely wholly on prepackaged foods. If it's possible, we think you should carry fresh foods rather than dried ones. When you don't have refrigeration facilities, or don't want to deal with excessive weights, plan meals with fresh food for the first day or two, then rely on the more durable and lightweight dried varieties.

Prepackaged freeze-dried dinners are readily available at most outdoor specialty stores. Many of these are excellent, and most of the ones we've tried weren't bad. Taste is such a personal thing that we can't recommend any particular meals, but we can advise

Prepackaged freeze-dried dinners—Photo courtesy of Alpineaire Foods

72

you to avoid meals with unrealistic serving sizes ("four 2-ounce servings" won't feed four people) and excessive packaging. We both have had good luck with products from Harvest Food-works, AlpineAire Foods, and Backpacker's Pantry, and we suggest you look for their labels to start out.

If you aren't interested in buying prepared dinners, you'll be happy to know that most of the foods you regularly eat at home can probably be made from readily available dry ingredients.

In addition, many foods that we usually refrigerate at home will keep for quite a while without refrigeration in not-too-hot weather. Hard cheeses like cheddar, fruit, peanut butter, nuts, seeds, salami, smoked bacon, butter, potatoes, onions, garlic, and anything pickled are all in this class of foods. Eggs will keep for a few days if it's reasonably cool outside, and so will soft cheeses and fruits, and most fresh vegetables. Most bread will keep fine for days, but it tends to get smushed. Rather than carrying plain old bread, try lots of crackers, or bagels.

If you need food that doesn't weigh much (for backpacking or day trips), apples, pears, bananas, and a few other fruits dry well and are readily available at most grocery stores already dried. Raisins and prunes are good, too, and are available almost everywhere. Pastas and many packaged dinners are also good for camping because they have long shelf lives, are easy to prepare, and are relatively light. Hard-to-find dried foods, like eggs and tomatoes, are often available at co-op grocery stores. Check out the one nearest you.

You might also consider purchasing a food dehydrator (about $60 and up) to make your own beef jerky, dried fruit and vegetables, and other taste treats.

Whatever food you decide on, you should make sure it can be fried, boiled, broiled, or eaten raw. Most camp cooking equipment doesn't allow enough variation in heat (they are, as we mentioned earlier, either on high or off) to allow gentle simmers, steaming, or much else; and, while baking on a camp stove or fire is possible, it's difficult so we won't discuss it here. Any baked goods you need to keep you happy when you're camping should be made at home before your trip begins.

Real "Trail Foods"

Although we generally stick to our normal diets when we're camping, we do enjoy a few traditional "trail foods" when we're out in the woods. These are things that we will not eat at home under most circumstances, but which we enjoy immensely when we're camping. Our recipes for these treats are as follows.

Bannock

(A traditional fried bread, easily cooked on a camp stove.)

To make dry mix for 2 (approx 8") pans start out at home by stirring together:

2	cups bread flour (or all-purpose white flour)
1 1/2	cups whole wheat flour
3/4	cup cornmeal
3/4	cup rolled oats
1/3	cup bran
2	tablespoons powdered eggs (optional)
2 1/2	tablespoons baking powder
1/3	cup liquid vegetable oil
1/2	to 1 cup powdered milk

Pack all of this in a reusable plastic bag. When you're ready to use it in camp, mix about half of the dry mixture with water—we're not sure how much as we've never measured it—until you have a stiff batter (or a soft dough if you like heavy bread). Pour the batter into a well-oiled frying pan and fry it on "medium," or as close to medium as you can get, for 5 to 15 minutes, depending on what you call medium, turn the loaf and fry it some more. Serve with peanut butter and honey.

Granola

Stir together:

8	cups rolled oats
1/4	cup brown sugar
1/2	cup wheat germ
1/2	cup shredded coconut
1/2	cup bran

Warm 1 1/2 sticks of butter (or 3/4 cup liquid vegetable oil) and about 1/4 cup honey in saucepan and add to dry ingredients. Stir well and bake on a lightly greased cookie sheet at about 300° F, stirring frequently, until golden brown (about 45 minutes). Add some raisins, dry apples and bananas, nuts, or whatever you like and store in a plastic bag or reusable container.

Serve cold with milk or warm by adding hot water to the cereal. If you're using powdered milk, you can avoid lumps by mixing the milk with the cereal before adding water.

Trail Mixes

Trail mixes, or gorp, are popular with campers and are available at many grocery stores. We prefer to make our own. These high-protein snacks can also be served for lunch in place of meat or eaten like a breakfast cereal.

Trail Mix I
Stir together:
$2^1/4$ cups roasted soy nuts
1   cup sunflower seeds
$1/2$ cup shredded coconut
$1^1/4$ cups rolled oats
1   cup rolled wheat
$1/2$ to 1 cup each roasted peanuts, dry apples, raisins
$1/2$ to 1 cup plain tvp (texturized vegetable protein)

In a saucepan, warm
$1/2$ cup liquid vegetable oil
2 to 4 tablespoons honey
$3/4$ cup peanut butter
Add honey mixture to the dry ingredients. Mix well.
Add powdered milk 2 tablespoons at a time until the mixture is dry. Store in a plastic bag or reusable container.

Trail Mix II
This is a simple mix and proportions may vary freely. Stir together roasted soy nuts, peanuts, shredded coconut, almond slivers, raisins, chocolate chips, corn nuts, and banana chips. Eat by the handful.

Packing Food

It's a good idea to take time to organize your food before you go camping. This makes life in camp much easier, and you might find

it's more fun to do the work before your trip than it is to do it during the trip. Packing food is work. It isn't really hard work, but it is work.

The first thing you want to do, when you've finished shopping for a trip, is to organize your dry food by meal. This takes four piles, one each for breakfast, lunch, dinner,

and "staples" (things you might use at any time). Pack all of your dry food in one- or two-quart heavy-duty plastic bags. These can be reused trip after trip. We prefer bags that don't have zip closures, so we close the bags by tying loose knots in the tops rather than relying on wire twist-ties which tend to puncture the bags. Instead of carrying a bunch of cardboard with you, remove all of your boxed food from the boxes, cut out the directions, and pack food and directions together in your plastic bags.

If you plan on carrying your food on the water, in a canoe or boat, double bag everything.

Once you get your food organized, pack each meal's food in a large stuff sack. A nylon laundry bag or plastic garbage bag works just as well. To avoid confusion, label the four large bags by meal, and the small ones—those with a single meal's ingredients—by contents. It isn't fun to mix up a batch of mashed potatoes thinking its pudding, while your camping partner adds the pudding to your stew.

If you're taking any fresh food along, pack it in a cooler for the drive to your campground. Freeze anything that freezes well (meat, cheese, butter, etc.) and use it in place of ice. Pack everything else in plastic containers. Keep everything in your refrigerator, rather than in the cooler, until you're ready to walk out the door.

You should not carry any glass containers. They always break. Also try to avoid metal containers (so it never matters if you forget your can opener). Too many cans get left in fire pits or in the woods, and they generally weigh more than the food they hold. If you're taking soda or beer, though, do carry cans—those nonreturnable plastic bottles don't get recycled often enough and don't compact easily for storage once they're empty.

Chapter 6

Under the Moon and Stars & Stuff
Trail Behavior and Techniques

Within reasonable limits, what you do when you're camping is really your own business—that is, as long as it doesn't infringe on anyone else's use of the campground or recreational resource. How you do things is definitely not only your business. Proper techniques will help minimize your impact on the environment. The only way you can really avoid doing *any* damage, of course, is to lock yourself in the closet, but that just isn't practical most of the time. Minimum impact techniques are the best alternative. That's the first reason you should practice the techniques of minimum impact camping.

A second reason you should practice minimum impact techniques is that they help you to not infringe on others' camping experiences, which, in turn, might keep others from infringing on yours.

Minimum impact techniques actually start before you go camping. At home, or any time you're not camping, you can take care to protect the environment by being an environmentally conscious consumer, conserving scarce resources, by minimizing your consumption of gas, electricity, and water, and by recycling everything you can recycle. Being environmentally conscious all of the time is a good thing in itself, and if you do these things at home, minimum impact techniques in the woods will be easy.

Your Impacts

We'll start with what we consider to be the most basic tenets of minimum impact camping, then we'll go on to address techniques.

The impacts campers have on the environment fit two basic categories. These are *sociological impacts* and *environmental impacts*. Sociological impacts are those effects that one individual's recreation activities have on another's. Sociological impacts include unkempt sights, distasteful smells, sounds, actions, and attitudes; unwanted or unwarranted intrusions; and any number of other human-to-human interactions. Most sociological impacts, we're convinced, result from a lack of respect and consideration for the rights and privileges of other human beings, or a lack of awareness of one's self.

Environmental impacts are those effects that your recreational activities have on the environment and all of its components. Wildlife (fauna), plants (flora), and soil are all living (biotic) parts of the environment; while air, water, and rocks are all nonliving (abiotic), but nonetheless important, parts. Anything you do that affects one of these components is an impact, whether it obviously "hurts" the environment or not. Some impacts might seem harmless, but the cumulative effect of even small changes to a localized animal-plant-land community can result in massive environmental degradation. You should, therefore, always try to minimize your impact on all components of the environment.

Littering is, perhaps, the most obvious and most discussed of the environmental impacts, but this category also includes a wide range of visual impacts, such as carving names where they don't belong, breaking branches off trees, uprooting plants, peeling bark, leaving fire scars, vandalizing campsites, and changing, in any way, the natural or groomed appearance of the environment in which you camp. Not all environmental impacts are visual.

Walking, driving, or biking off hardened trails can compact the soil. Soil compaction can kill plants by destroying their roots, it can create erosion problems, and it can kill a variety of flora and fauna that depend on uncompacted soil.

Carving in, breaking branches off, or peeling bark from a tree can open it to all sorts of fungal infestations or insect parasites that can, eventually, kill the tree.

Picking too many berries can kill a mouse and for want of a mouse, a fox may die, and for want of a fox, the kingdom may fall. Improper toilet procedures can contaminate a river. Improper use of soap may alter the plant, oxygen, and fish populations of a lake.

The impacts humans have on the environment are far too widespread and interactive to list completely. All we can say is that anything you do when you are camping can have an impact and may eventually destroy a much wider area than at first may be apparent. Minimum impact camping is the best way we know for you to minimize that effect, without having to keep out of the woods altogether.

The Real Basics

We believe a few things not usually included in discussions of camping techniques and skills are very important no matter where you camp. These most basic skills include your group's size and behavior, and your personal attitude.

Group Size

When you go camping, it is important to keep your group small. We prefer to limit parties to six because that's the number you can fit comfortably into two four-person tents and almost comfortably into two larger two-person tents. Some of our colleagues feel that eight or ten is a more appropriate maximum group size. Whatever number you choose, remember that the size of your group influences both your environmental and your sociological impacts.

The sociological impacts of large parties are obvious. Anyone who has ever gone to a big beer bust or a church picnic ought to be aware of how much noise and activity a crowd can generate. Because people go to the woods to escape that sort of commotion, it is best for you, too, to leave it at home.

The environmental impacts of large versus small groups is a topic we love to avoid. We like to believe that we know large groups have more of an impact than small ones, but evidence from research suggests that active small groups can have as much impact as lethargic large ones. Whatever the research suggests, intuition should tell you that more people will equal more, or at least more widespread, impact on the environment.

Group Behavior

We've already mentioned that we think it's wise to avoid high-use times and areas, unless you have a reserved campsite. This is for your comfort as well as for the comfort of other users. It can also reduce your immediate impact on wildlife (which doesn't want to see you nearly as much as you want to see it) and will help prevent overtaxing campsite resources.

You can easily minimize your social impact by avoiding contact with other groups. When this isn't possible, keep your contacts limited in space and time. Many people are far too polite to tell you to go away, even if they wish you would. If you want to get to know someone you meet camping, get their phone number and call them when you get home; you should generally stick to yourself in the woods.

You should also be careful not to exceed the limits of your ability, experience, and education. You will be less likely to have accidents, and then you won't have to interrupt another group to ask for help.

In addition to all these other things, you should keep a low profile. Avoid wearing bright colors and skirt open areas, fields, and such on the trails—especially when other groups are near. Don't bring a portable TV or boom box camping with you. Don't throw wild parties. Don't stay up all night shouting or howling at the moon.

Basically, what we're saying here is be cool, lay low, and don't get into other people's space.

If you are backpacking or day tripping, always rest well away from trails, public sources of water, and scenic areas. You aren't the only one who wants to use those scarce resources, but you'll be the only one who can if you set up house, even a short-term one, on top of one of them.

Personal Attitude

Some topics seem to call out for ambiguous, indeterminate discussions. This seems like it might be one of them.

Whether or not you enjoy yourself, your activities, and those of the people with whom you are camping is your own business and no one else's. On the other hand, whether you act like you are or aren't enjoying yourself might be someone else's business.

When you agree to go camping with other people, you become, in part at least, responsible for them. It is impossible not to inter- act with, influence, or seriously annoy anyone with whom you are sharing a tent. It seems important, then, to control your behavior.

You should always at least pretend to have a positive attitude, even if you don't. A positive attitude, even a feigned one, can help you maintain positive social interaction with your companions, it can help insure open communication between and among group members, and it can prevent one person from ruining a trip for everyone.

It is customary to complain about the food and weather, howev- er, so go ahead and gripe about them a little in a good-natured way.

Camping Skills

Camping skills start with your selection of a campsite and run through most of the things you'll do to make that site more com- fortable. We address what we consider to be the most important skills first and then deal with the others in something approaching the order that you will encounter a need for them on-trail.

Campsites

In most organized campgrounds, you'll either be assigned a site or you will take your pick from a limited number of prepared or hardened campsites. If you go somewhere where this is not the case, in an area where camping is allowed, make sure you camp well off any trails and away from local scenic attractions. Just like rest spots, other people may want to use the water or see the sites.

Isolated shorelines really aren't as good a choice for campsites as conventional wisdom suggests. Transitional environments, like the shore of a lake, the edge of a field or forest, or the foot of a mountain, tend to have more wildlife and more diverse ecosys- tems than other parts of the local environment. If you camp in the middle of a transitional zone, your environmental impact will be magnified.

Pick a site well shielded by trees, plants, and/or geography, so other groups don't have to look at you change your shirt—and so you don't have to look at them either. You will also be considerably less visible if you avoid using brightly colored equipment. A green or brown tent can blend right into the scenery, while an orange one can't.

Keep the number of tents and other shelters in your site to a minimum and put clotheslines and other visual intrusions well out of sight of any public areas. No one, we're quite sure, wants to watch your laundry dry.

If a prepared or previously hardened site is available, use it even if you don't have to. Most of the negative impacts that result from camping activity occur in the first few days of use. It is hard, almost impossible, to crash a site (that is, camp where no campsite previously existed) without having some impact. It is relatively easy to leave a used site better than you found it.

Do not cut or move live vegetation or standing deadwood, even if it's right where you want to put your tent. Something almost always lives in or off of standing dead wood, and the plant called "dibs" (we heard it!) by virtue of getting to the spot first. Besides that, in most places you can go to camp it is illegal to cut any live plants or standing deadwood. They are integral parts of a number of species' habitats and they deserve to be left alone.

Don't trample vegetation or compress soil through excessive activity. We realize we haven't defined excessive, and we're not too sure we can, except in a situational sense—our situation, that is. A full-scale soccer match, it is fair to say, is excessive anywhere off a game field, but five trips to a tent and back might not be too many. The point is that some moving around in a campsite is natural and fine, but try to keep your wanderings to a minimum.

Don't engage in construction or landscaping activities. It is fine for you to landscape your yard and you can lash together anything you want in your bedroom, but don't do either of these things in a campsite. Don't make rustic benches from fallen logs, either, unless you can (and do) put the logs back where they came from as soon as you are through with them.

84

If you aren't using a prepared or hardened site, move your campsite at least every two days and your kitchen area every day. Any longer than this and no matter how careful you are, you will begin to have visible and detrimental impacts. Little trails hither and yon, dead plants where your tent blocked the sun, animals permanently frightened away from their homes, and similar effects are easier to avoid if you don't hang around too long.

Keep your campsite clean. Apart from preventing inadvertent littering, a clean campsite is less likely to attract bears or other scavenging animals than is a messy one. With sweet-smelling food, salty clothes, and other smelly rubbish strewn about, how can the animals resist? Many human messes can also prove toxic or accidentally fatal to a wide range of curious animals.

Setting Up Camp

While you might not have much choice where you set up camp, how you set up is almost entirely up to you. It is also an issue of style—either you'll have it or you won't.

Most drive-in campsites come equipped with a level "driveway" area. These areas make a great place to park your trailer, if you have one, or your car, if you don't (have a camper, that is). If you want to be stylish, you'll back your vehicle into the drive; this makes it easier to get to the trunk and eliminates any temptation to use the headlights in lieu of a flashlight or candle lantern.

Set up your kitchen on and around the picnic table, if one is provided, and on level ground away from delicate plants if a picnic table isn't provided. If you're in a drive-in site, you might like to keep your kitchen near the trunk of your car, so you can use it like a pantry; in other sites, use your tarp as the kitchen cupboard. During hot weather, you might want to keep your kitchen on the east side of a tree or large boulder, so it will be in the shade during sunny afternoons.

You should, of course, put your tent on the smoothest, most level piece of ground you can find within the confines of the campsite. Before you set up the tent, though, make sure there are no large tree branches hanging over the area where you want to put it or any trees nearby that might fall on you while you're asleep. Being rudely awakened by an aspen falling across your back is not, we can assure you, a desirable experience.

You might also look at the area around your proposed tent site to be sure water will flow away from your tent when, or if, it rains. Many campgrounds are kind enough to provide groomed tent sites, so this procedure is often quite easy.

It's sometimes nice to use a waterproof tarp as a "ground cloth" to help keep you dry inside your tent in very wet weather. If you want to do this, make sure the tarp is slightly smaller than the tent floor and use it inside the tent. If you put your ground cloth outside the tent, water can pool between it and the tent floor and might soak through into your sleeping bag. Also, if all the dust and bits of leaves you carry into the tent on your clothes fall onto a tarp rather than the floor of the tent, it's easier to "sweep" up in the mornings—just roll up the tarp, carry it outside, and shake it briskly.

Once the kitchen is arranged and the tent has been set up, you should concentrate on hanging your hammock (if you are so inclined) between two sturdy trees or between the bumper of your car and one sturdy tree; finding the area's toilet and water facilities (where you can fill your water bladder and do whatever you need to do to any other bladders); and making sure your equipment and clothes are organized and easily accessible. If you do all of these things before you start to play, you won't have to worry about getting them done later.

Food & Food Wastes

If you read the section on food, you know that we think all of your food should be prepackaged in reusable containers or plastic bags. If your containers are all reusable, it is easy to remember to carry them all back home; but even if they aren't reusable, if you carried it in, you also have to carry it out.

We strongly recommend that you do not take glass bottles or cans on your trip. These containers are prohibited in some places—the Boundary Waters Canoe Area Wilderness for one— because wherever they're used, they often end up as litter. Even in developed parks, where you can try to prevent litter by using trash cans, animals will drag things out of the garbage bins. It is also likely that any recyclables that you throw away in a park or campground will end up in a landfill. So, if you do have non-reusable containers and no on-site recycling facilities are available (it never hurts to ask if they are!), wash your containers, take them home, and recycle them yourself.

Never bury used food containers of any sort, or food, or anything else not covered in the human waste section below. If you bury it, something will dig it up. Don't try to burn food scraps, either, because it takes a very hot fire a long time to burn most foods.

Do not try to burn used food containers or packaging. You can burn uncoated paper, like tissue paper, because it burns quite easily. But, the coated papers, Styrofoam, and plastics used to package foods tend to shrink up into hard little balls of refuse that won't ever burn completely in a small outdoor fire. They also tend to release toxic fumes when exposed to heat, and most campsites don't have smoke scrubbers.

If you cook things that require boiling, you'll need some place to dispose of the leftover water. Quite a few campgrounds provide sinks for such eventualities, but not all of them do. In those that don't, you'll need to dig a sump hole.

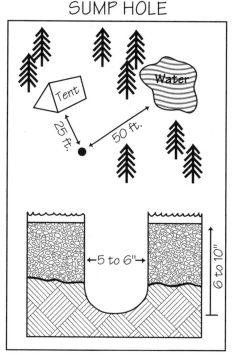

SUMP HOLE

A sump hole is, as the name suggests, a small hole in the ground into which you put "sump" (or is it sumps?). You can dig one of these holes by taking your trowel and very carefully removing a small piece of sod from a spot in the campsite at least 50 feet from any water source and at least 25 feet from your tent or kitchen. Then start digging. A hole with a diameter of about five to six inches will generally be sufficient. A sump hole should be dug into the mineral soil—the grainy layer of sandy soil that usually starts about six to ten inches below the surface and runs down to bedrock—so that everything you dump into it drains out of the local ecosystem.

Only fluids should go into this sump hole. It's good for draining pasta, washing your contacts, and brushing your teeth, but not for disposing of leftovers.

Because small holes tend to get bigger the more you use them, and because the soil you removed to create the hole tends to disappear after a while, you should close your sump hole every day as soon as you're through using it (after brushing, before bed). Fill it in carefully and replace the sod intact. If it isn't raining, sprinkle some water over the hole so the sod can recover. If you do this right, no one will ever know where your sump hole was.

Do not wash your pots or dishes in lakes or streams (or any other body of water). Food in the water is a pollutant, and it's a really ugly sight for the next person who uses the site. Generally, all you need to do to wash up is to rinse your dishes with warm water and sterilize them by boiling. Soap will get them shinier, but soap residue is a frequent cause of all sorts of intestinal problems like diarrhea and is really hard to get rid of. If you don't use soap, dishwater can go into the sump hole. If you use soap to wash your dishes and no sink is available in the park, you should wash them at least 150 feet from any water source, according to the procedures outlined in the next section.

Eat or pack out (in your garbage bag) any food remaining in the pots after your meal. Only liquids (or mostly liquid residues) should go into the sump hole, or down the drain if you have a sink. We repeat, don't throw food out with the dishwater!

Lastly, do not feed the animals. We realize that this is cliche and that not feeding those cute little red squirrels may make them move over to the next campsite, but animal diets and human diets aren't comparable, and you don't, or shouldn't, want nondomestic animals dependent on the presence of humans for their survival. If the animals get too used to the junk-food diet provided by campers, they may also lose access to other sources of food (they forget them or other animals take over the territory). Camper dependent critters have trouble surviving when all of the campers go home.

Soap

We really do think that you should avoid using soap in any non-urban (wild or wilderness) environment. Not using soap for a year or two might make you smell like a real mountain person, but a few days of abstinence shouldn't hurt too much.

You should avoid using soap in a camping environment because it negatively affects the environment, and because cleanliness is, well, so godly. Camping is supposed to be fun and not entirely decorous. If you do use soap, use it carefully and sparingly.

Any soap you use when camping must be biodegradable. Castile soap fits this description, as do any number of other readily available soaps. Biodegradable means that living agents in the environment (biota) can degrade, or break down, the ingredients of the soap into inert elements.

Biodegraders almost all live in soil rather than in water. It is, therefore, important to clean bodies, dishes, clothes, and anything else you want to clean somewhere where the wash water will not reach the lake, stream, creek, river, or water table without first passing through a lot of soil. A sink or shower intended for washing, with drainage into a septic field or tank (or a sewer system) is, of course, the only place you really ought to use soap. But, you can also use it in a pot or other container at least 150 feet from any lake, stream, or other source of water. If you empty the pot where you use it (well away from the water), the wash water and soap will end up in the soil where soap can biodegrade.

This really is important!

Imagine washing your hands in a full coffee pot. Doesn't that sound fun? Now, drink the coffee that's in it. Gross, eh? Well, that isn't too different from using soap directly in the water. Even biodegradable soaps are pollutants! They can also fertilize all sorts of algae that most people, and many fish, would rather avoid.

Human Wastes

Most places that allow camping provide flush toilets, outhouses, or pit toilets (outhouses without walls). These are sometimes not the best facilities, but it is important that you use them. If, for any reason, you can't use one of these toilet facilities, you should follow the rules outlined below.

Urinate at least a few feet off of any trail, for privacy, if nothing else and at least 50 feet from any water source.

In wilderness areas, or when you are stopped for a rest on a day trip, your latrine area must be 150 to 200 feet or more from any water source and should be out of site of any campsite or scenic attraction.

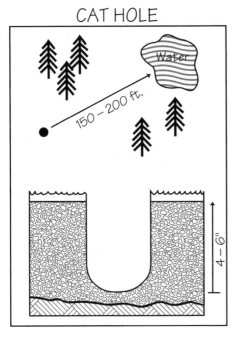

CAT HOLE

Where toilets aren't available, you should use cat holes (single-use latrines for bowel movements) about four to six inches deep, in organic soil rather than mineral soil, to allow for easy decomposition. Organic soil is richer and darker, more like potting soil than the sandy, granular organic soil underneath it. Cat holes are better, for environmental as well as aesthetic reasons, than the group latrine pits some guides recommend. These small holes should be closed (that is, refilled) as soon as you are through with them.

You really should pack out all of your used toilet paper, but if, for some reason, you can't, you might carefully burn it before closing cat holes or leaving the latrine area (that's one of the reasons we recommend you carry a lighter). Toilet paper will decompose, but not quickly, and nothing is grosser than little piles of used t.p. scattered throughout the woods.

Do not bury food waste, sanitary napkins, tampons, or bandages in your latrine pits, or put them in pit toilets. Food wastes should be placed in your garbage bags, and the rest can be carefully burned in an existing fire pit, or wrapped and packed out with the garbage.

No-trace Check-up

The last of the basic tenets of minimum impact camping is that the leader of any group (you, your mother, father, brother, or whoever) must personally check every campsite and rest area used by the group to make sure that all traces of the group's use of the site have been eliminated. This is called a no-trace check.

Make sure that there are no new fire scars, litter, or leftover equipment. Make sure that all latrine pits are sealed and that the sump hole is filled and the sod replaced intact. If you haven't already done so, replace moved objects like stones or logs in the positions they occupied when you borrowed the site. Pick up all the visible litter, then look for more—we have almost never used a site that didn't have at least one tent stake, a couple of candy wrappers, and a half-dozen twist-ties (all left over from some other group's use) hiding in it somewhere. Scatter any leftover fire wood in the woods. Check carefully for any other signs of your use, and do what you need to do to erase them.

"Take only photographs, leave only footprints" is not too original, but it is an accurate expression of what you should try to do in your camping environment.

No Trace Check List

✓ No new fire scars   ✓ Sump hole filled
✓ No litter   ✓ Sod replaced
✓ No left equipment   ✓ Replace moved objects
✓ Latrine pits sealed   ✓ Firewood scattered

Hanging a Tarp

The easiest way to set up a tarp is to buy one with poles and follow the directions on the package. If you don't want to spend extra money on this option, you'll need to develop other techniques. We have two that we use quite often.

The first one is to take a tarp with parachute cord attached to its corners and stretch it evenly between four trees (one, of course, for each corner) by tying the parachute cord to the trees about four feet off the ground. Take a canoe paddle, or any other straight pole about five feet long (or longer), and pad one end with a neatly folded bandana. Place the padded end of this pole in the center of the tarp and put the bottom end on the ground. This should leave your tarp stretched tight enough to shed water and should leave enough room under it for you to cook and eat comfortably. If it does, then be impressed with your own creativity and camping abilities.

This first set-up is quick and easy, but it is often not too stable. Besides, four suitable trees are often hard to find. That's why we prefer technique number two, or any variation on it.

Start by running a piece of parachute cord between two trees, or any other stable objects, about four feet off the ground. Hang a tarp across it like a sheet. Secure the middle edges of the tarp by tying them to the parachute cord or to the trees from which it is hanging, then stretch one end (the back) away from the center at a sharp angle—try for about 45 degrees. Tie the "back" corners to trees at or near ground level, or stake them to the ground like the corners of a tent. Stretch the front away from the center, too, and tie it off on two more trees, but keep it almost parallel to the ground so that you can get under the tarp without a struggle. You should make sure to set this little tarp shelter up so that any wind is blowing toward its back end, or your mealtimes might be uncomfortable.

Either of these methods can be used to hang a tarp over your picnic table or kitchen area, and it is probably not a bad idea to do so. Mealtime is just loads and loads more fun if you can get out of the rain to cook and eat.

Knots

Any knot that you can tie, and that won't slip when you want it not to, will work in most situations. You are free to use your own knots and not feel guilty at all, but be aware that some knots are better than others.

Three things make a knot good: the ease with which you can tie it, its ability to hold without slipping, and the ease with which you can untie it. The most useful knots for campers are probably the bowline (which is pronounced *bo'lin*), the overhand knot, the figure eight, and the half hitch. All of these are easy to tie once you know how, they all hold well in appropriate situations, and they all are easy to untie if you've used them correctly.

Unfortunately, it's much easier to demonstrate knots than to describe them, and we can't do any real demonstrations or practice sessions here because it's a book. Nonetheless, we'll try to explain these few knots anyway.

We'll need to start the explanations with two definitions.

The "tail" of a rope is the end nearest the knot; usually it is also the short end.

We call the rest of the rope the "line," or the longer portion of the rope.

Half Hitch

A half hitch is not really a knot. It's only half of one. Take one end of your rope in your left hand. Pass the tail (the end) around an object (a tree, for example) and take hold of it with your right hand. Pass the tail under the line, which should be on

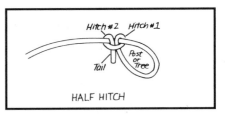

HALF HITCH

the left side of the tree, bring it back over the line to the right, and pass the tail through the space between the rope and the object. You should have a half hitch. Two of these make a serviceable knot. You can use this knot to hang your hammock or a clothesline from a tree, to secure anchor lines to anchors, and to connect ropes to a whole bunch of other things. Hitches are sometimes hard to untie, though, so you might consider leaving a loop (like the bow you leave in your shoelace) on the second half hitch.

Overhand Knot & Figure Eight

The overhand knot is used to tie loops into the middle of ropes for climbing and near the end of a rope for many other purposes. You can tie one quite easily. Make a loop in the rope by folding the tail back toward the middle of the line. Hold both strands in your left hand, take the loop at the end of it in your right hand, fold the loop over the top of the two strands in your left hand, bring your end loop under the two strands, and tuck it up through the new loop you've created. Pull it tight. Now, if you wrap the loop all the way around the two strands and tuck it down through the new loop, you get a figure-eight knot, which is much easier to untie than an overhand knot.

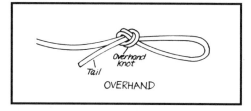

OVERHAND

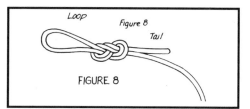

FIGURE 8

Trucker's Hitch

If you need to tie a taut line between two trees, you can secure one end of your line to a tree with a bowline, or two half hitches, and then secure the other end with a trucker's hitch. This extra knot is really a combination of the first two.

To tie a trucker's hitch, bring the tail end of your rope around the tree from

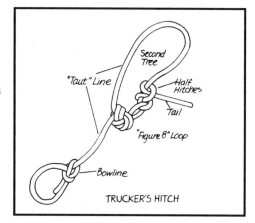

TRUCKER'S HITCH

the left to the right and pull it taut. Pinch a spot on the line about 12 to 18 inches from the tree and let everything go. Tie an overhand loop, or a figure-eight knot, in the line so that the spot you picked is at the end of the loop. Pass the tail back around the tree and through this loop, then pull the tail toward the tree. When the line is taut, tie the tail off with a couple of half hitches.

Bowline

The bowline is a much more complicated knot and might be hard for you to tie. Don't worry if it is, as you can camp quite easily without ever tying one. It is easiest for most beginners to tie one around their waist, so that is how we'll explain it here.

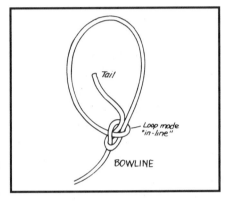

Pass one end of your rope around your waist working from left to right. If you do this correctly, you'll have the tail end of the rope in your right hand and the main line in your left one. Hold both ends of the rope with your palms up and thumbs on the outside. Without letting go of the tail, put your right hand (palm down and thumb toward hip) on the main line next to your left hip, grasp the line with your right thumb, and turn your right hand away from your body to make a loop in the line. Hold the loop in your left hand. Run the tail of the rope, still in your right hand, up through this loop, pass it under and around the line on the side of the loop away from your body, and pass it back down through the loop. Pull tight. If there is a knot in your line, it's called a bowline. The bowline is really useful for hanging things because it doesn't slip and is relatively easy to untie.

A Note on Knots

If you really want to know how to tie a variety of useful knots, take a class in climbing. If you can't take a class and want to learn from a book, get a Boy Scout manual. The Scouts explain knots really well.

Fires & Firewood

The first rule for fires is try not to use them at all. Firewood is renewable, but not quickly so. So in heavily traveled areas, you really should use a stove and candle lantern in place of a fire. If you do plan on having a fire, in spite of this strong recommendation, the rules for burning are fairly simple.

Rule two is to use fires only for cooking unless you are in an emergency situation and need a fire to keep warm or to signal for help. You really don't need fires for anything else—if you get cold, clothes keep you warmer than flames, and you should have a candle to sit around at night if you want a focal point for your activities.

Rule three is that you can only have cooking fires where and when they are permitted by local regulations.

If there isn't already a fire ring or pit where you are camping, use your stove—don't build a new fire ring. If you do, the chances are good (like 100 percent) that you'll leave an unsightly fire scar. There is also the possibility of setting the top layer of the soil, which is usually made up of small bits of plant and wood, on fire.

Firewood is easy to carry in the trunk of your car. Unfortunately, it is illegal to transport wood between provinces in Canada, across the border between the U.S. and Canada, or between some of the various states. That may be why a number of parks prefer you to buy your wood on-site at the camp store. If you can't buy wood on site and didn't (or couldn't) carry it with you in your car, consider using charcoal instead of wood.

If you're camping away from a car and need to collect wood in the woods, you should remember the four "d"s.

The first "d" stands for down. Anything still standing is not firewood or even potential fuel. It has to be all the way down, on the ground.

The second "d" is dead. Anything alive has a right to continue that way.

The third "d" is dry. This should be obvious, as wet wood doesn't burn well. By dry, we also mean that any down, dead, dry wood will do. It isn't necessary to find all pine or maple or birch for your fire. If it will burn, you can cook on it.

The last "d" is distant. You should start looking for wood at least 75 yards (a completely arbitrary figure; you could make it 100) from your campsite. Too many people burning the closest deadwood can clean out the forest near a site in a matter of days and make that site wholly unattractive to future users.

You should also follow the "rule of thumb" when you are searching for wood. If a stick is thicker than your thumb, leave it lie. Small "twigs" burn quickly and don't leave a lot of ashes or coals. Rather than relying (as many writers advise) on a bed of hot coals, you can cook over a roaring twig fire. It works fine, doesn't make too much of a mess, and doesn't deprive a lot of fungi, moulds, and insects of the larger deadwood they need to survive.

The last rule is to make sure that your fire is completely out when you're finished cooking. The only way to do this is by feeling it with your hand. If it burns you, or even if it's warm, it isn't out. Use plenty of water, stir, feel, and then use more water, just to be sure.

Scatter any unburned wood well away from your site and don't leave a bunch of coals or garbage in your fire pit. You can scatter the former in the woods and carry the latter in your garbage bag.

Lighting a Fire

If you insist on lighting a fire, you should at least do it the right way. Generally the right way is also the easy one. (While we're on the subject, did you ever read Jack London?) All it takes to build a fire is some wood and enough heat, applied carefully of course, to start the wood burning. Sufficient heat is easily provided by a match or lighter and some paper or other easily combustible material. Dousing your potential fire with gasoline is unnecessary and quite dangerous.

The easiest way to get a fire going is to light some charcoal, by following the package directions, in the fire pit and then pretend there are comforting flames. You can also cook on the charcoal, and then add wood until it really has flames and looks more like a traditional campfire.

The second best way is to light a fire from scratch.

Birch bark, or so conventional wisdom tells us, is the best tinder available. As we know, though, conventional wisdom isn't always too accurate. This time it happens to be close. Birch bark is a really good tinder. So, if you happen to find bits and pieces of birch bark laying around on the ground, there is no reason not to pick them up and use them. If, on the other hand, the only way for you to get this substance is by peeling it off trees (which, as we've tried to explain, you can't ethically do), then proceed without it. Crumpled newspaper, or almost any other dry paper, works just fine anyway, and so do small dry twigs, dry pine needles or cones, really crispy leaves, or small wood shavings carefully carved off a stick.

To light a fire, put your crumpled paper or other tinder in the center of the campsite's fire pit. Take a bunch of small twigs (pencil sized and smaller) and build a loose tepee-shaped mound over the tinder. Using your lighter or a match, light the tinder. Protect the small flames from strong winds with your hands or a plate, and gradually add more small twigs until a hearty flame is blazing. Gradually increase the size of the twigs you're adding for fuel. You might find it appropriate and necessary to add oxygen to your fire during this process by blowing a thin stream of air at the base of the flames or by fanning it with a plate or bellows.

The stump of a small candle will serve in place of crumpled paper on cold or wet days, and you can buy little fire starters (napalm-like tablets or pastes) that will enable you to get most anything combustible combusting; but, as we keep saying, you don't really need a fire anyway, so why bother with one at all?

Map & Compass

Maps are generally clear symbolic or pictorial representations of the terrain (land features and human additions) and should make sense if they are oriented to the same direction as the land. Compasses are made so that you can easily match your map's orientation to the world's. The two are intended to be used together, and that's why this section is called "Map & Compass."

Most maps are printed so that true north, that is the north pole is at the top of the paper. You can make sure yours is by looking at the legend or key, which is usually printed on the bottom of the map. A directional arrow somewhere in this key should show which way north is on the map, and it should also show some-

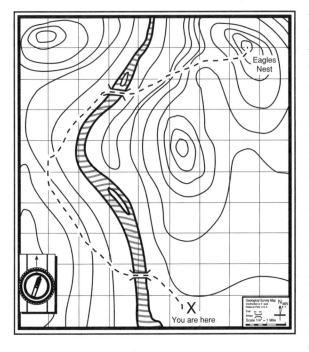

Eagles
Nest

X
You are here

Geological Survey Map
Declination is 5° east
National Park U.S.A.
Trail
Bridge
Scale 1/4" = 1 Mile

N MN

thing called magnetic north (MN) or list the map's declination in degrees east or degrees west.

Now, look at your compass. If you hold it level, and away from any metallic or magnetic masses, the colored (almost always red) needle on your compass should point to magnetic north. Magnetic north is the center of a large magnetic field located somewhere north of Greenland. Unless you are directly south of this field, true north (map north) isn't exactly the same as the north on your compass. The difference between these two norths is called the declination. In the Boundary Waters Canoe Area, the most popular wilderness area in the United States, the average declination is about 2 degrees (which is close enough to zero to ignore, so if you are in northern Minnesota, skip the next few lines). West of a line that approximates the Mississippi River, the declination is measured in degrees east, and east of the line the declination is measured in degrees west.

Refer to the legend or key on your map to find out what the declination is, in degrees east or west, where you're camping. If the compass has an adjustable declination setting, follow the manufacturer's directions to set it appropriately. Otherwise, hold your compass firmly by the base plate and turn the housing (the dial) until the printed north arrow (or 0 degrees) is aligned with the direction-of-travel arrow on the base plate. Now, turn the housing to the right if your declination is east, and to the left if the declination is west, carefully counting the number of degrees that pass the direction-of-travel arrow. When you've turned the dial the same number of degrees as the declination, the printed arrow on your housing will point to magnetic north when the direction-of-travel arrow on your base plate points to true north. Now you can orient your map.

Put your map down on a flat, level surface. Make sure that no nails, screws, bolts, or large chunks of metal (including rocks with a high metallic content) are directly under the map or near your compass. Put your compass on the map so that the direction-of-travel arrow on the base plate points to north on the map. You can usually do this by aligning the straight side of the base plate with the edge of the map. Turn the map and compass together until the red arrow and the printed arrow on the housing, or 0 degrees on the dial, are aligned. Your map is now oriented and features on the map should clearly represent features you can see in the real world. If you do all of this at a trail head, the trail printed on the map and the one you're standing on should point in the same direction, and you should be able to navigate it safely. If they don't, check your work, and do it again.

If your map is properly oriented, you should be able to follow it quite easily by translating right and left, forward and back from the map into real-world directions. If you can't, stay in camp or on well-marked trails.

If you don't have trouble translating directions from map to world, you can even consider leaving the trail (regulations permitting, of course). Before you do, though, make sure you know which direction to go (use your compass) to get back on it—or to a road, a body of water, or some other large landmark that will safely lead you home.

Most compasses come with basic directions. Read them, too, and make sure you understand how to use a compass before you rely on one as a navigational aid.

If You're Lost

If you don't use your map and compass well enough, you might get lost. Try not to, but if you do, don't panic.

The worst thing you can do if you are lost is to wander around hoping you'll find your way. Most people walk in circles when they do that (conventional wisdom isn't always wrong!) because they step farther with one leg than the other.

The best thing you can do, if you get lost, is to ask for help. If someone is nearby, walk over to them and ask where you are; pride shouldn't stand in the way of finding your way home.

If, as is usually the case, no one is in sight, it's time to use your whistle—the one we've suggested you wear all the time. Sit or stand next to a tree you like, introduce yourself to it and apologize for being noisy, and blow away. The traditional emergency signal is any loud noise in groups of three (three bursts of three on the whistle, pause, three bursts of three, and so on). Keep blowing 'til help arrives. If you don't have a whistle (you should always have one, though) shout, but pause more or you will get so hoarse you won't be able to make a sound. You can also try pounding a stick against something hollow or smacking two large rocks together, but neither of those is quite as effective as a whistle.

Cleaning Water

The value of clean water should be self-evident. Clean, potable water is important because you can't survive very long without it. Although "drinking the water" is probably not, as conventional wisdom holds, the number-one cause of the "trots" (soap residue left on pots and dishes after washing probably earns this status), most untreated water sources still aren't safe to drink.

If you can't carry water from home and aren't sure the camp area's water supply is free of parasites, you should treat your water. Boiling water for at least five minutes will make most water potable, and chemical treatments should work if you follow the directions that come with the treatment. But neither boiling nor chemically treating water is as effective as filtering. Any filter capable of removing giardia cysts, which have a diameter measured in microns, should also filter out almost all the other nasty fauna and flora. If you want to play it safe, buy and carry a filter with mesh 1.0 microns or smaller, and use it according to the manufacturer's directions. A more detailed discussion of water treatments is provided in our discussion of water filters in Chapter 3.

Weather

Predicting the weather is not, by any stretch of the imagination, an exact science. Nonetheless, the best way to do it is to listen to the inexact scientists who predict the weather for the evening news. If you can, listen to the news on the radio and take into account the professionals' predictions of probable patterns (nice alliteration there, eh?) in the weather when you are planning your camping outings. Once you're actually camping, you probably won't have easy access to a radio (unless you ignore our advice and carry one), so you'll have to remain aware of the weather without any assistance from the news. You can do that by watching the sky and by noticing if you're cold or hot.

Most sorts of weather shouldn't affect your camping fun. You can deal with heat by taking clothes off, cold by putting them on, and rain by wearing your rain gear. It will help, though, if you have some idea about possible changes in the weather before they happen. You have to be particularly alert to the possibility of storms, as lightning and strong winds require special care and more protection than is generally provided by a raincoat.

Cloud formations are often pretty, and they are also reasonably good indications of potential weather changes. While it might be fun to know all about stratocumulus and other such clouds, all you really need to remember is that big fluffy clouds mean partly cloudy skies (nothing to worry about), and dark ominous clouds mean possible storms.

The wind, too, can help you foresee the weather. The prevailing winds blow most all the time. If the wind shifts to the direction opposite the prevailing wind, expect a change in the weather. This is not 100 percent accurate, but it should caution you to be alert. If you are alert to changing conditions, they're generally easier to deal with.

The safest way to deal with severe weather, such as lightning or a wind storm, is to get inside a sturdy building. If there is no inside to go to, you should look for low ground, away from any tall objects (like big trees) that might attract lightning or get blown over on top of you. Gullies and ditches are good. You don't want to be in the water, though, during an electrical storm.

Dealing with less severe weather merely requires adequate and appropriate clothing, plenty of food and water, and a good attitude. A little sunshine is nice, but you don't need it to enjoy camping.

Loading Your Day Pack

Loading a pack is really a personal thing. There is no one right way to do it; however, there are a few basic guidelines that will make your pack more comfortable to carry. Day packs and the larger frame packs should really be loaded in a similar manner, so you can follow these directions for backpacking too, only the number of items will differ.

You'll find that packs are easiest to carry if there are no sharp objects poking you in the back, so put your sit pad or some other soft object into the pack first and make sure it stays closest to your back. If you're carrying a tarp, blanket, towel, or air mattress, it can be used for padding, too.

Bulky, lightweight items go in second, right on the bottom of the bag. In most cases, an extra sweater or shirt foots this bill. You should always carry at least one extra sweater or a bunting jacket, and the bottom of your day pack is as good a place as any.

The heavy stuff should go on top of the large bulky items. If you don't have side pockets big enough to hold a water bottle, it should go in the middle of the day pack, as close to your back as possible. Food, a stove, books, and any other heavy things should go there, too.

Your first-aid kit should go into an easily accessible outside pocket, if there is one, or else you have to put it on top of the food and such.

Your sunscreen, windbreaker, map and compass (if those aren't in your hand or pocket), pocket knife, cup, water filter, lip balm, flashlight, extra socks (optional), use permits, wool hat, necessary toilet articles, and toilet paper should go in next, wherever you can fit them.

The last thing to go in, so it is easily accessible, should be your rain gear. Don't forget to carry it all the time you are away from your car or campsite—you never know when you'll need it.

A Word on Fishing

Fishing is great, and we think you should fish if you want to. Just make sure you have the appropriate license. You should also make sure you dispose of fish entrails properly.

Like any other food waste, it is best if you put fish entrails in the garbage. If you object to that, and regulations allow it, you can bury fish entrails in a shallow hole at least 50 yards from any campsite. Do not throw them into the lake. It might be tempting to "feed the turtles," but throwing remains of fish in a lake might affect it negatively. The decomposition process can deplete the oxygen supply in cold lakes, and it might contribute to all sorts of other problems, so do not do it.

Protecting Your Food

If animals are a problem in the campground you're using, the managers will know. Follow their advice and lock your food up at night. If you have to, hang it from a tree.

Hanging food from a tree is easiest if you don't have too much of it. This is another reason to eat heartily. Start the hanging process by putting all your food into a plastic bag and then seal that into one pack or a sturdy food bag. Tie the middle of your quarter-inch rope around the pack. Find two trees 12 to 15 feet apart that have branches about 15 feet off the ground. Throw one end of the rope over one of the tree's branches and the other end over the other tree's branch. Working from one end of the rope, pull the pack up until it is 8 or 9 feet off the ground. Tie this end of the rope off on the tree or a nearby boulder (or a person who won't be moving before morning). Then, take the other end of the rope and pull the pack even higher. This should also pull it away from the tree and leave it hanging at least 10 feet off the ground and 6 feet away from any trees. Tie this end of the rope off on something solid, too. Thus hung, your food should be safe from almost anything.

Some campsites provide bear-proof cages for food storage. If yours does, use it. Others provide bear poles (bars between two posts or trees) that make it easy to hang food well off the ground. If neither of these amenities are provided, follow the procedure outlined above and hope that your food pack is intact come morning.

In black bear country, if you do get a nocturnal visitor, and blowing your whistle doesn't make it go away, give it your site. You can't win an argument with a 300-pound bear.

If you are in grizzly country, check with the park managers about appropriate precautions before you even consider camping out.

Protecting Your Person

When you're camping, you really do have to be careful to avoid accidents and injuries. Of course, you should be just as careful at home. There are, however, at least three things campers have to be particularly careful to avoid. These are dehydration, insect-borne diseases, and poison ivy. Several friends have suggested that we comment on them here, so we shall.

As we mentioned in an earlier chapter, dehydration can be a serious problem for campers. When you're out in the woods, you expend a lot of energy and expel, through sweat and respiration, a lot of water. To avoid getting dehydrated, adults should drink three to four quarts of water every day. Don't rely on "feeling thirsty" as a measure of your need to drink because it won't work. Just drink a lot, often. If you're getting enough water, your urine will be clear; if it isn't, drink more.

A number of insects can cause you problems, but most of them fall under the category of "local hazards". You can get information about them from rangers or other resource managers. One little bug, though, is more than local and really is becoming a camping problem.

The deer tick, *Ixodes dammini*, is a tiny insect only about 2 to 4 mm long (that's 1/16 to 1/8 inches, if you can't do metric). It is a reddish brown color, darker towards the tail than the head, and it can carry Lyme disease.

Lyme disease usually starts with a round, clear-centered rash around a tick bite and looks like a target, and in mild cases it can cause symptoms much like the flu. More severe symptoms include inflamed joints, stiff necks, headaches, facial paralysis, meningitis and encephalitis-like neurological symptoms, and heart blocks. If it is identified early enough, this disease is usually easily treated with tetracycline, but it is even more easily prevented.

You can avoid tick bites by wearing long pants, tucked into your socks, and long-sleeved shirts whenever you are in the grassy areas ticks frequent. A bit of tick repellent on your clothes doesn't hurt either. You should also check yourself frequently for ticks and remove any you're carrying ASAP. If one does bite you, it might not be a bad idea to check with your doctor when you get home.

Deer Tick

Size comparison to Wood Tick

Adult Female Deer Tick

Average Wood Tick

female

0   1

Actual Size Inch Scale

Poison Ivy

Poison ivy is a plant you should avoid touching as its oil can cause all sorts of rashes and nasty itching. The leaves are made up of three leaflets with jagged edges and reddish veins, its berries are ivory colored, and its stem looks rather woody. If you think a plant might be poison ivy, it might be poison ivy, so treat it as though it is.

Being Good & Careful

We deliberately did not include here any information on pitching a tent, lighting a stove, and other basic activities because you can get more specific directions with the equipment when you buy it. We also omitted tips on using an axe or saw because we think that they should be made illegal for use outside private homes. In fact, most parks prohibit all cutting, effectively making their use illegal anyway. Anything else we forgot will probably come to our attention soon and will be included in future editions.

Some of our tips are more important when you're camping away from your car and the potential comforts it provides. We realize many people never do that, but we think it is important that people choose to camp in trailers or cars because they want to do so, not because they don't know any other way. Besides, almost everything that applies to a five-week trip in the wilds of Montana also applies to a one-day trip in a county preserve. The wilds are as much in our perceptions as they are any place else.

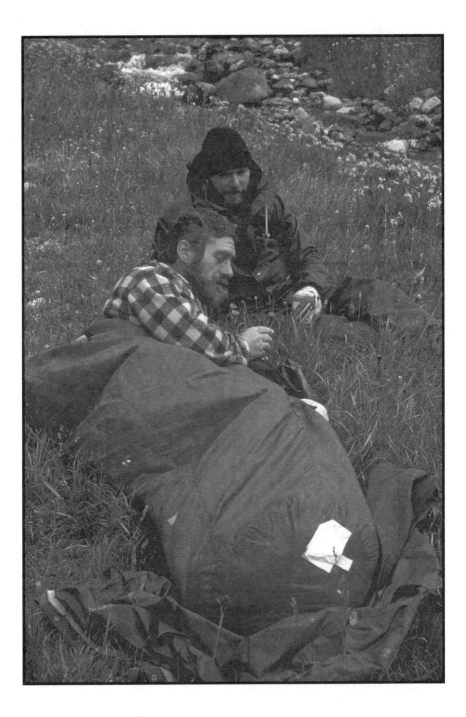

Chapter 7

Beyond the Pale
Trip & Canoe Camping

Most of the techniques discussed thus far in this book are intended to help you camp out of or near your car, or a related motorized vehicle. We have focused on vehicle-based, organized campground camping because we assume—correctly, we think—that most camping in the state, and even in the National Parks, takes place in drive-in campgrounds.

Be that as it may, not everyone is content to stay near the car. The "pale," the borders of our civilization, are clearly an attraction for many of us. Sometimes it is important for our peace of mind for us to step beyond those borders and into the wild backwoods; sometimes we do it just for fun. Whatever the "why," we do do it often. Consequently, we have decided to include a bit about back-woods camping.

For many centuries, the "backwoods" of North America have been accessible to trippers by foot (mostly on land) and by canoe (mostly on water). While the wilds are now accessible on horse-back, by car, motorcycle, motorboat, and by a hundred other means of transportation, we're really quite conservative and are only going to talk about the two traditional means of backcountry transportation.

Canoeing

Canoe tripping seems to be the most easily learned extension to camping in the parks, and it also seems to be one of the most easi-ly accessible. There are many hundreds of canoe "trails" on state and federal wild and scenic (and recreational) rivers, on state and county designated waterways, and in a few protected wilderness areas. Basic canoeing skills are also really easy to learn.

While there should be enough information here to get you moving in the right direction, keep in mind that this is a short guide that contains far less information than most of the popular books about canoeing skills. It is not, by any stretch of the imagination comprehensive; it is, rather, a very brief introduction to the art of canoeing. The guide, at least this chapter of it, should help you to identify some of the skills you need to learn and practice, and provide some of the information you need in order to get away from the campground on an overnight canoe or backpacking expedition. Only time, energy, and a great deal of practice will make you a real expert on the subject. Start small, work your way up, and you will have it down pat in only a few years.

On the brighter side, this chapter contains all sorts of bizarre words, and it might actually help you to improve your performance at Trivial Pursuit™.

A Bit about the Canoe

The first thing you ought to do now (for your gaming enrichment) is to learn a bit about canoes and water.

"Canoes," in the broadest sense of the word, come in a variety of lengths—anywhere from under 10 feet to over 30 feet—and a whole bunch of bizarre shapes, like those monsters with flat backs for mounting motors or specially designed racing hulls; however, specially sized, designed, or modified versions of the canoe require discussions of their own. So, in this work, the word "canoe" refers exclusively to a narrow boat from 16 feet to 18 feet long—the typical, average, normal work-a-day, man-in-the-street canoe with more or less pointed ends, two seats, and a middle about three feet wide—which is intended for general recreational use.

The Parts of the Canoe

The canoe is a remarkably well-designed boat. Its shape enables it to move easily through the water. It is very maneuverable, and most canoes are easy to transport. Someone, somewhere, sometime must have done a lot of experimenting (and probably a lot of swimming, too!) before hitting on the design we

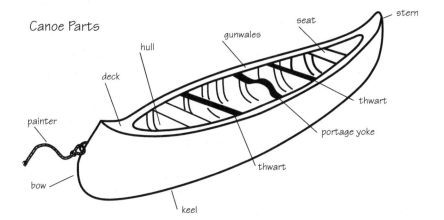

Canoe Parts

now recognize as your average canoe. Anyway, while the canoe is not as fast or as stable as, say, an 18-foot tri-hull with a 200 HP Merc inboard, it is fast and stable enough to get you around, and it is certainly more useful than the tri-hull when it comes to overnight canoe tripping. Before you are qualified to judge an opinion like this one, though, you better learn a bit about what it is that makes a canoe a canoe.

If you haven't got a canoe sitting around to look at now, try reading this while you're sitting in a bathtub full of hot water. Tubs are comfortable and familiar to most, so we'll try to equate the parts of a canoe to your average household tub.

The top edges of a canoe's hull (or the edge of the tub where you're resting your elbows) are usually called gunwales (pronounced "gunnels"—probably for the same reason bowline is pronounced "bo'lin"). If you want to get real technical, the term "gunwale" is actually a generic reference to the strips of wood, plastic, or metal attached to the hull, while the term "outwale" refers to the outside strip, and the term "inwale" refers to the strip on the inside. The top edge of the hull is, so far as we know, called the top edge of the hull. Gunwales (or out- and inwales) help add stability to the canoe's hull and—especially if they're made of mahogany or Sitka spruce—can be very pretty to behold.

Attached to the gunwales, you'll generally find two or three "thwarts"—those inch or so wide strips that run across the canoe behind the front seat and in front of the back seat—which also help the canoe hold a stable shape. In most canoes you'll also find a pair of seats. Canoes that are going to be portaged (carried on your shoulders between lakes or streams) usually have a "portage yoke" in place of the center thwart. This yoke is a strip of wood, plastic, or metal attached to the gunwales at the middle of the canoe. You can identify it by the C-shaped curve in its middle (so it will fit comfortably around the back of your neck). The yoke sometimes has pads for your shoulders on either side of the curved part.

Since bathtubs usually don't have seats, yokes, or thwarts on them anywhere, that analogy probably won't work too well. We're real sorry if we got your hopes up.

The hull of the canoe (since we hate to lose an analogy completely—that would be the most tublike part) is often stiffened laterally, from side to side, by "ribs"—not unlike your own—attached to the inside bottom of the boat. The hull probably will also be supported by two small "decks." The decks are those little ledges on the front and back of the canoe that seem to also be perfect handles for carrying the boat from place to place.

Many canoes use a keel to help stiffen the boat longitudinally (that's lengthwise). The keel is a long strip of wood, plastic, or metal on the outside bottom of the boat that always gets caught on rocks and logs when you don't want it to. While the keel is primarily a structural device, it can also help the canoe to "track," or move in a straight line, when you're paddling.

The front of the canoe (where the spigot is on your bathtub) is called the "fore" section, if you are referring to the space inside the canoe, or the "bow," if you are referring to the front of the canoe itself. The back is called the "aft" section (spatially) or the "stern."

"Painters"—lines or ropes of various types—may be attached to the bow and stern of the canoe. Many canoes (especially fiberglass and aluminum ones, which don't naturally float if they are full of water) may also have some sort of flotation device under the two, fore and aft, decks.

You should now be able to define all of the following words. Be sure to remember them well.

Canoe Vocabulary Words
List One:

aft	bow	deck	fore
gunwale	hull	inwale	keel
outwale	painter	rib	seat
stern	thwart	track	yoke

These aren't all the strange nautical terms associated with canoes. If you learn to use these few, though, and to apply them to the right parts of the boat, you can really impress your neighbors even if you never learn to paddle at all, and you can probably get by in most conversations about canoes. If you don't want to get away from the campground but like the social status that comes from a powerful vocabulary, just learn the terms and skip the rest of the chapter.

Canoe Materials

Canoes can be built successfully from any number of different materials. The most common for rentals seems to be aluminum, which doesn't make bad boats. Some rentals and most of the boats you can buy are made from various and sundry other materials including plastic (most commonly Uniroyal's ABS™ or one of the variations on polyethylene), fiberglass, wood, and other more exotic laminated fibers, like Dupont's Kevlar™. We'll work through the characteristics of each material in turn.

Wood Canoes

There are three general types of wood canoe: wood and canvas, wood-strip hulls covered in fiberglass (very pretty), and plain old wood not covered with anything. We've never paddled, and only rarely seen, the last of these three types; and the second variation is really a fiberglass hull, so we won't talk about either of them here at all.

With its wood plank hull and ribs with a canvas cover to keep the water out, the wood and canvas canoe is a less expensive and more easily constructed variation on the ancient birch-bark canoe. Few methods of water transportation, according to Curt, are more aesthetically pleasing or appeal more to one's sense of history and romantic notions than a canvas-covered white cedar canoe almost just like the ones the voyageurs paddled. Although wood and canvas are among our favorite canoe construction fibers, not a lot of people paddle wood canoes any more because they are heavy, expensive, and not commonly available for rent. A lot of our friends like to look at them in museums and at boat shows, but very few of them are willing to paddle one. Beauty really is in the beholder's eye.

Wood boats, as we mentioned, are expensive (starting at over $1000) and delicate. No wood canoe we've ever encountered will stand up to many direct hits on rocks or submerged logs, and canvas, or even birchbark, covered hulls won't stand up to much abrasive contact with dry ground. They are also, as we mentioned, very heavy, weighing 80 pounds or more. Even if the beauty and allure of wood boats really rocks your socks, we can't recommend them for beginners or occasional trippers.

Fiberglass Canoes

We really don't know a whole lot about fiberglass technology and most of our emotional reactions to fiberglass boats were formed by outdated monoliths that weighed about 120 pounds and floated about as gracefully as a bathtub does when the house floods. Such boats have created a whole generation of canoers afraid of fiberglass.

Fortunately, technology has changed and fiberglass boats have improved considerably in the past 20 years, so we'll tell you a bit of what the manufacturers tell us about today's fiberglass canoes.

Fiberglass is an amazing hull material. It can be easily shaped into almost any form and makes sharply defined, clean, and sleek hulls. Fiberglass hulls are pretty (our opinion, as we like the way the glass shines). Fiberglass hulls are constructed by layering sheets of fiberglass fabric on forms and coating the sheet with a hardening resin. Sometimes a wood form is used between the inside and outside layers of the hull. Many of the "build your own canoe at home" kits use this method, and these quasi-wooden canoes can be especially beautiful. A number of other materials

116

are also used to fill the middle layer of fiberglass hulls, both to stiffen them and to add buoyancy. Fiberglass boats are generally coated with something to protect the shine and to help make them more abrasion resistant.

Fiberglass is relatively stiff and brittle, which means that 'glass boats are not as impact resistant as the plastic ones. For canoeing on lakes and calm rivers, the speed and ease of motion of the sharp fiberglass hull makes it a good, moderately expensive ($600 and up) hull material. Continuing with this bright note, we'll add that the modern fiberglass boats are lighter than the monsters of yesteryear, and they now tend toward the moderate end of the scale in weight (60+ pounds), making the lighter 'glass boats popular on trips with lots of portaging.

Plastic Canoes

Plastics and their attributes vary a great deal, so we have chosen to focus on the two most commonly used in canoe construction—ABS™ (Acrylonitrile Butadiene-Styrene) and polyethylene. Both of these plastics are used, like fiberglass to make laminated hulls. The hulls typically have foam cores to add to their strength and buoyancy.

Uniroyal's ABS™ is an exceptionally tough and forgiving fiber. Canoes made from ABS™ can be (almost literally) wrapped around rocks without breaking, unlike fiberglass or wood. They bounce right back into shape. This almost amazing flexibility makes it difficult to puncture these hulls unless you try really hard. Neither of us have ever actually tried to wreck an ABS™ hull, but a guy we know once paddled his Royalex™ (Old Town's ABS™ material) canoe over a small waterfall. We don't consider this a good idea, but as far as we could tell, he hardly damaged the boat (or his body) at all.

ABS™ materials will tear if you really give them a chance — nothing is indestructible—and it requires some specialized knowledge to repair them, but their durability makes ABS™ boats a good choice if you aren't sure about your ability to dodge rocks, and if you don't mind paying for durability (at $600 and up, they are moderately expensive). These canoes tend to be heavier than fiberglass ones, and you may not like carrying them from place to place. On the other hand, you may not mind at all.

Polyethylene canoes, like ABS™, are flexible and, for the most part, forgiving. They are also very abrasion resistant. Polyethylene canoes are like a low-cost radial tire when compared to the top-of-the-line ABS™ versions; they are a less expensive, but certainly useful, alternative and are good for everyday use. Polyethylene canoes are a bit less durable than ABS™ boats, but they are also less expensive ($350 and up). They tend to be in the moderately heavy weight range.

Kevlar Canoes

Fiberglass, plastic, and Kevlar are used to make laminated hulls—layers of fabric held together with resins. Kevlar™ is Dupont's name for a natural fiber about which we know, in a technical sense, next to nothing. We do know that Kevlar™ is used in astronauts' suits, in bulletproof vests, as a reinforcer in some plastic and fiberglass canoes, and also in some extremely lightweight (40 or more pounds) and durable canoes.

Kevlar™ is not as resilient as plastic. If you wrap a Kevlar™ boat around a rock, for example, it won't spring back into shape. But it is tough as nails and hard to wreck under most conditions. Like fiberglass, Kevlar™ can be shaped into really sleek hull designs, so these boats tend (assuming they are well designed) to paddle beautifully. Their light weight makes Kevlar™ boats easier to portage than most others, but the cost ($1000 and up) is hard for the beginner to bear.

Aluminum Canoes

For as long as we can remember, aluminum canoes have been the standard for resorts, outfitters, and rental agencies everywhere. Aluminum boats are relatively inexpensive ($400 and up), durable, abrasion resistant, and easy to repair. On the other hand, the material is hard to shape into sleek hulls, so aluminum canoes tend to be clunky. They are also heavy (60 to 80 pounds) and not at all chic.

While aluminum may not be as stylish as some other materials, it isn't a bad choice for the beginner.

118

Hull Design

Two general hull characteristics should be of interest to the neophyte: hull size and hull shape. Size is easier to explain, so we'll start with that.

Canoes shorter than 16 feet and longer than 18 feet aren't much use for normal tripping. Smaller boats won't hold enough, and larger ones are too heavy and awkward for the beginning tripper. Because canoes turn around their middle, shorter boats are easier to turn, while, conversely, longer ones are easier to keep moving in a straight line. Because beginners often need help going straight, a length between 16 and 18 feet is the first thing to look for. Seventeen feet, give-or-take a few inches, is pretty much the standard for basic tripping canoes.

Hull width, measured in the center of the boat, is important. Standard-length boats range from about 29 to about 38 inches in width. Wider hulls provide primary stability—that is, they make the canoe relatively stable when it is sitting upright in the water—but because a canoe has to push water aside to move forward (or backwards, as far as that goes) and because the width of the canoe helps determine how much water has to be pushed out of the way, wide canoes are harder to paddle than narrow ones. Most of the boats we paddle on trips are about 36 inches wide.

Depth, again in the center of the boat, is the last dimension that need concern you—unless you can find a four-dimensional boat (ever watch "Dr. Who"?). Standard depths range from 12 to 15 or 16 inches in the center. Deep hulls have more freeboard (the portion of the hull above the waterline) than shallow hulls, and are, as a consequence, more seaworthy. They usually hold more people and gear. On the down side, deep hulls can make it hard for you to reach the water, and the extra freeboard increases the boat's wind resistance. Deep hulls can be harder to paddle and harder to control in strong winds than their shallow counterparts. If you are planning to carry lots of gear, or to paddle on a wavy lake, go for a canoe at least 13 inches deep.

Hull shape is so complicated that you really need a course in engineering to get past the basics. We recommend beginners look at the general shape of the canoe (nontechnically, how streamlined it is), the shape of the keel line (lengthwise across the bottom of the boat, where the keel goes if there is one), the amount of curve, from side to side, on the bottom of the hull below the waterline, and the amount and direction of side to side curve on the hull of the boat above the waterline.

The most streamlined racing canoes have very sharp bow lines (or "entry lines") and widen smoothly and gently from the bow to just beyond the canoe's midpoint. Generally, tripping canoes will not be too streamlined, because aluminum and plastic—the most commonly used materials—are hard to shape into real sharp bows, and because a canoe that is wide over much of its length is more stable than the narrow, gently widening ones. Trip canoes are also usually widest right at the midline (that is, their hulls are symmetrical), while the streamlined ones are widest slightly aft of the midline.

The keel line of a canoe (when viewed from the side) can be flat, or it can turn up slightly at the bow and stern. This curve is called "rocker." Canoes intended for paddling on flatwater (like lakes) have little or no rocker because the flat keel line helps keep the canoe tracking easily. Canoes built for whitewater (rapids) have lots of rocker, because the more the hull curves upwards towards the bow and stern, the easier it is to turn.

If you intend to paddle on rivers a lot, you might prefer a boat with a little bit of rocker. This will make it easier to turn quickly. For the same reason, you might also prefer to paddle a boat without a keel, because the keel tends to resist turning and is prone to catching on rocks and things you will most likely be trying to avoid.

The shape of the center of the hull, when viewed from the front, is called its cross section. The portion of the cross section below the waterline can show a flat bottom, a curved bottom, or a "veed" bottom.

Flat-bottomed boats feel real stable in calm water—this, if you remember, is called primary stability—and are convenient for fishing and other activities that require easy access to lots of gear. Flat-bottomed hulls, though, have very little secondary stability. Even though they feel stable on calm flatwater, they are easily flipped by waves or by quickly shifting loads.

Canoes with rounded bottoms work the other way around.

They feel real unstable in calm water, that is, they have poor primary stability, but are relatively hard to tip over (ergo, they have good secondary stability).

Canoe designs aren't like principles, however, and you should always be willing to compromise on your design, at least with respect to cross sections. General recreational use requires a versatile hull design, and a little compromise can provide that versatility. A gently arched bottom or a "veed" hull are probably the best bets for most general-use canoers. A gentle arch, being not quite flat and not quite rounded, provides both reasonable prima-

Basic Canoe Designs

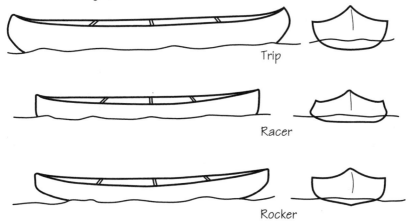

Trip

Racer

Rocker

ry and reasonable secondary stability. "Veed" hulls are a simple variation on the gently arched one. They combine an arch with a protruding "vee" that is very much like a keel built right into the hull, rather than one that is added to it later.

The portion of the cross section above the waterline can either be flared out or curved in. These two characteristics are called, respectively, "flare" and "tumblehome." A flared hull helps deflect waves and adds secondary stability. It also makes it harder to paddle right next to the hull. Tumblehome adds secondary stability and makes it easy to paddle right next to the hull (which is important for improved control), but it won't deflect waves at all. Some boats use a combination of the two, but we can't really say if that offers any advantage.

For general use, you might find you prefer a gently arched hull

121

and a bit of tumblehome on your boat. The latter is important partly so you have an opportunity to work the word "tumble-home" into your conversations (it sounds so silly) and partly so you can conserve energy by paddling right next to the hull. As with everything else for the out-of-doors, you'll have to try the canoe to see if its design suits you.

This brings us to our second set of vocabulary words. We hope you haven't forgotten the first set already, because before we begin the new set, you are required to complete the section I quiz. You now have four minutes to recite and define the first ten words on the vocabulary list. Begin now.

Canoe Vocabulary Words
List Two:

arched bottom	bow/entry line	cross section
depth	flare	flat bottom
keel line	length	midline
primary stability	rocker	round bottom
secondary stability	tumblehome	veed
width		

That was just fine; stop reciting now and read on.

Choosing a Boat

If you opt to rent a canoe for tripping, you probably won't have much choice in materials or design. (We say probably, because you can rent almost anything somewhere, but most rentals are still aluminum.) Even if you are renting, you should still take a moment to consider the canoe's design and materials, because both can be important for safety, and safety is always important.

Because we don't know where you are planning to paddle or what you plan to do on the trip, we can't really recommend a particular kind of boat. We can, however, say that Grummun and Alumacraft both make reasonably priced, durable, and relatively versatile aluminum canoes. If you aspire to be a gear-head (a group of campers who express the philosophy that "it doesn't matter if it's over priced and trendy, as long as it looks good"), you may want to avoid aluminum boats on aesthetic grounds—

they make too much noise when you hit rocks in the water and trees on portages (not that you'll ever do that), and also when the metal flexes in the water. If such is the case, spring a few extra bucks and rent a plastic boat.

Since we seem to have been involved in offering something approaching endorsements throughout the previous chapters, we might as well go all the way and say that we are especially fond of Mad River Canoes, and we like Old Town a lot, too. Both of us think the Kevlar™ Mad River Explorer is the best general-use boat on the market, followed closely by the ABS™ Old Town Tripper and it's smaller copy, the Crosslink™ (polyethylene) Old Town Discovery 169.

In fairness, we should also admit that We-no-nah makes some pretty sharp boats out of fiberglass and Kevlar™. We're sure that a number of other companies do too, but we can't say so for sure as we've never paddled their boats.

Paddles

Paddles, like canoes, come in a whole bunch of shapes and sizes, and—sort of like widgets and knuter valves—everybody has different names for the same parts. In our own nomenclature (the one we've been using throughout this book), the parts of the paddle are the "butt" or "grip" (otherwise known as the handle), the "shaft" (or long, skinny part), the "throat" (where the shaft meets the blade), the "blade" (that wide part at the bottom that goes in the water), and the "tip" of the blade (the bottom edge of the paddle).

The type and shape of paddle you use, and its length, should be determined by what kind of canoe you are using and where you are using it. Realistically, though, the type and shape of paddle you

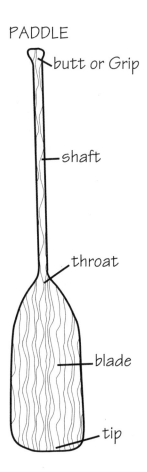

PADDLE

butt or Grip

shaft

throat

blade

tip

use will be determined by whether you rent or buy your canoe. If you are buying, you can select a paddle for tripping use by considering three things: blade width, shaft length, and materials.

In most cases a blade width between six and nine inches is more than enough. Too wide a blade will make it difficult for you to paddle, and too narrow a blade will make it easy to paddle but hard to move the canoe anywhere in a hurry. Both of the paddlers in the canoe should have paddles with blades about the same width.

The length of a paddle is really a matter of taste and technique, but in general, the paddle should go from the top of your foot to somewhere between the top of your sternum and your chin when you are standing normally and the tip of the paddle is resting on your foot. We both prefer paddles that reach the top of our sternums when sized by this method. You can also choose an appropriate length by sitting upright on the floor. With butts (yours and the paddle's) on the floor, the throat of the paddle should be just about even with the top of your head. If we're not mistaken (and we rarely are), this latter method is the better, and the more trendy, of the two.

When it comes to materials, we're not really sure what to say. Plastic and aluminum paddles—that's a plastic blade and butt, and an aluminum shaft—are popular with renters because they are all but indestructible. They are also relatively inexpensive ($12 and up). Wood paddles can be really cheap or really expensive ($8 to $100+) and are every bit as good as the material and workmanship that goes into them. Some of the newer paddles are composites. These tend to be very lightweight, very strong, and very expensive ($80 and up).

If you do buy a paddle (not a bad idea if you'll use it a lot—even if you rent the canoe), keep in mind that weight is important whatever material you choose. On a normal day of paddling, you'll lift your paddle about 50 times a minute every minute you paddle, so you are well advised to look for one that weighs in at two pounds or less.

Durability is also important. We'd guess that the phrase "up the creek without a paddle" didn't get its meaning for nothing. That's why the generally strong plastic and composite paddles are so popular, and also why the better wood paddles often have synthetic tips.

Paddles are getting more and more complex every day. It used to be that all paddles were pretty much alike, but now you can get all these different materials and a number of different blade shapes. You can also buy bent-shaft or straight-shaft paddles.

For some strange reason, we generally recommend that beginners stick with simple, straight-shaft paddles, even though we've been assured by some serious enthusiasts, that the bent-shaft ones are more efficient and easier to handle. (For whatever it's worth, we really do like straight shafts better than the bent-shaft ones. Bent-shaft paddles are designed for racing, not recreational use.) With somewhat better reasons, we also recommend that beginners stick with a "beaver-tail" blade that is slightly rounded at the bottom, as this simple shape has kept canoers happy for generations and can be used effectively in almost any water.

If your paddle is the right size, you can easily get used to almost any shape, so don't worry too much about the minute details of your paddle's construction as long as it feels good, and looks good, and it will stay in one piece 'til your trip is over.

Life Jackets & Safety Devices

It would be remiss of us not to raise the issue of life jackets about now. For your edification, we should mention that life jackets aren't really called "life jackets" at all. They are properly called Personal Flotation Devices (PFDs), and they are a must for everyone in the canoe (the Coast Guard and the American Red Cross, and every other safety-conscious organization in the country, say so). Novice canoers and non-swimmers should wear (on their person, as

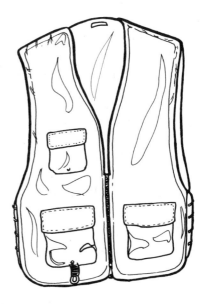

opposed to off it) a type II or type III PFD at all times when they're in a canoe and on the water, and anyone who can't turn themselves over in the water (because of age, physical disability, a tendency to faint when immersed, or any other reason) should wear a type I PFD.

Because a PFD is not real effective unless it is sized correctly and worn properly, you should try yours on over the clothes you'll be wearing in your canoe. You also must always use all of the zippers, clips, and belts on the thing according to the manufacturer's directions.

You can buy all sorts of Coast Guard approved PFDs these days, but we recommend you get a good vest style ($25 to $60) because they are more comfortable than the old "horse-collar" style and more effective than floating seat cushions. If you do have a vest-style jacket, try to keep it dry (unless you fall into the water). A dry, inch-thick foam vest can be very warm when worn under a raincoat or windbreaker, and you can also use one as a pillow at night.

While we are on the subject of life-saving devices, we will suggest that it isn't a bad idea to carry a throw line in every canoe to aid in rescues. A throw line is a brightly colored, 50- to 60-yard-long line kept packed in a stuff sack so it won't be tangled when you need it. A 20-foot coil of nylon rope, which many people carry in place of a proper throw line, won't work nearly as well as the real thing, so consider investing the $20 or so that the outdoor store charges for one, and carry it.

Paddlers should also wear polarized glasses on sunny days. This will make it easier to see obstacles under, as well as above the water and might prevent some eye problems, too.

Sunscreen and hats can help protect paddlers and passengers against nasty sunburns, and if they are fashionably designed (the hats, not the sunscreen), they can make you look really good. Never, ever, ever wear a hat that clashes with your canoe. Such faux pas can really get you into trouble with the fashion police.

Knee pads (those things kids wear when skate boarding), while not actually a safety device, are a blessing if your butt gets sore. With pads on, you can kneel on the keel, the bottom, of the boat, quite comfortably, for hours. Kneeling also makes your boat more stable by lowering its center of gravity.

126

Role of the Paddlers

Most 17-foot canoes will hold three people and their gear. But, for a number of safety reasons (like, a desire to not tip the boat) only two people, those sitting in the bow and stern seats, should ever paddle the canoe. Anyone else in the boat is a passenger.

The stern (back) paddler determines the general direction of travel; in quick maneuvers the bow might help with this. The stern paddler should be proficient in the forward or power stroke, back paddling, draw and pry strokes, and the basic steering strokes—the "C" and "J" strokes or the Maine guide stroke, or, if you can't learn to paddle, ruddering. In flatwater, the stern paddler has almost sole responsibility for steering. In whitewater, the stern paddler should be able to follow the bow's lead around rocks and other obstacles. The stern paddler also serves as captain, as the back seat does hold the tiller, and everyone else ought to follow her or his orders. (What we're saying here, is that canoers should be back-seat drivers!)

The bow (front) paddler provides about 60 percent of the boat's motive power. On nice clear routes this is easy, and the bow paddler can enter a trancelike state known affectionately, by a good friend of ours, as "the bow zone" or, by one of us, as the "O-zone." When in this state, the bow is allowed to be totally nonresponsive and need not pay any attention to where (in a general sense) the canoe is going. No matter what state she or he is in, though, the bow does have to watch for obstructions.

The bow should always watch for submerged rocks, logs, and the like, but in dark or murky water she or he might not sight these obstacles soon enough for the stern paddler to turn around them. Consequently, the bow should be proficient in some close-quarters maneuvering strokes (the draw and pry), as well as in the power stroke and backpaddle.

The duffer—the canoe's third person—is, as we've said, a passenger. The design of most canoes makes it impractical for the duffer to paddle, and having the passenger sit up to help does little but improve the chances of capsizing. That said, this passenger should be content to enjoy the ride and to serve as navigator, story teller, and personal servant for the rest of the crew.

The Strokes

Because we've already mentioned a few different strokes, we feel obliged to explain our terms. We'll try to be brief and to the point.

There are many different strokes—almost as many as there are canoers. Most paddlers, though, can get by with only a few, and by remembering that canoe paddles are designed to propel a boat by pushing against water. Always try to use these or similar strokes rather than using the paddle as a pole for pushing off solid objects.

Feathering

The motive strokes include the forward or power stroke, which, not surprisingly is used to move the canoe forward, and the back stroke or back paddle, which moves it in reverse. These strokes work best with your bottom arm, the one nearest the blade, kept straight and used as a fulcrum. Your top arm should be used to

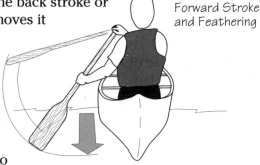

Forward Stroke and Feathering

push the butt of the paddle away from (in forward) or pull it towards (in reverse) your chest, in a line about 45 degrees away from the top of your sternum and angled down towards the gunwale of the canoe. Put the whole blade in the water when you're paddling, and on your recovery—when you have the blade out of the water—turn the outside edge of the blade toward the front of the canoe so the blade is parallel to the water. This is called feathering. It cuts the wind resistance of your stroke and helps save your energy for when you really need it.

There are a wide range of steering strokes, but only a few are really necessary under normal conditions. Here are the six steering strokes that we find most useful.

Draw Stroke

The "Draw." Reach out (away from the canoe) with the blade of the paddle and pull (draw) it in toward the canoe in a line perpendicular to your direction of travel. In the stern, this turns the canoe away from the side on which you are paddling; in the bow, it turns it toward the side on which you are paddling.

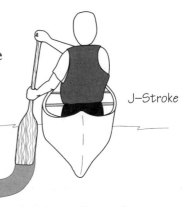

Draw Stroke

canoe turns

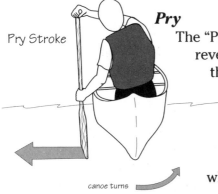

Pry Stroke

Pry

The "Pry." This is essentially the reverse of the draw. Put the blade in the water next to the canoe and push it away from the hull. In the stern, this turns the canoe toward the side on which you are paddling; in the bow, it turns it away from the side on which you are paddling.

canoe turns

J–Stroke

The "J–Stroke." This stroke is only used in the stern of the boat, and it should be used frequently to turn the canoe toward the side on which it is used to make small corrections in course. To "J," start with a normal power stroke, but as your bottom hand nears your hip, begin a "J"-shaped motion away from the hull and toward the bow of the canoe.

J–Stroke

This is easiest to do if you grip the butt firmly and turn the hand holding the butt forward until the thumb is pointing toward the floor of the canoe.

129

Ruddering

"Ruddering". This is another stern technique. It serves the same purpose as the "J," but it is less efficient as it tends to slow the forward progress of the canoe. To rudder, hold the blade of your paddle in the water at about a 30-degree angle from the side of the canoe and use it as a tiller. This, of course, only works if the canoe is moving forward in the water.

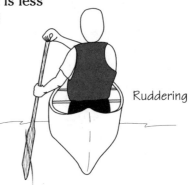

Ruddering

Maine Guide

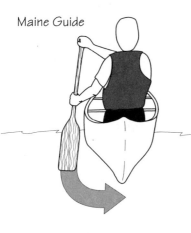

Maine Guide

The "Maine Guide". This stroke is another variation on the "J." Start with a power stroke, and when your bottom hand nears your hip, turn your paddle into a ruddering position.

C–Stroke

The "C–Stroke." This one is also almost exclusively a stern stroke and, like the "J," is used to make small corrections in course away from the side on which it is used. To "C," you start a power stroke but, as your bottom hand nears mid-thigh, you make a "C"-shaped swing away from the canoe and back in toward the stern. Because the "C" has its open side facing the canoe, it might be easiest to pic-

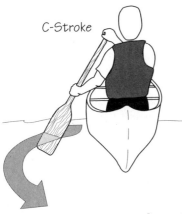

C-Stroke

ture this as a combination power stroke and draw.

Whatever strokes you use, we recommend that you always have your bow and stern paddlers work on opposite sides of the canoe. This maximizes your efficiency and minimizes the probability of your tipping over. Also, paddle in unison with a nice, steady pace; it looks prettier and works better than if the two of you paddle to the beat (pardon us, Henry David, for twisting this metaphor) of different drums.

Your last set of vocabulary words are here now. Memorize them, and you'll be a better person. To avoid having them fall into unfriendly hands, eat this page when you're finished.

Canoe Vocabulary Words
List Three

back stroke	beaver-tail	blade	butt
draw	J–Stroke	Maine guide	paddle
PFD	power stroke	pry	rudder
shaft	throat	throw line	tip

More about Safety

Safety comes up a lot in this book because it is really important. If you aren't safety conscious, you can easily get hurt. While this is as true at home as it is on the trail, it's a whole lot easier to get help if you're hurt at home. Because very few campsites come equipped with telephones, you can't call "911" from them, and accidents and injuries can become more severe than they might seem. Besides, any pain makes canoeing a real drag. With that thought in mind, we offer the additional following guidelines for safe canoe tripping.

1. Travel with at least two, and no more than three, boats in a group. Two gives you someone to watch and be

watched by, but more than three makes for messy and destructive camping.

2. Always carry an extra paddle in your canoe, just in case one breaks or floats away.

3. Be wary of large waves. It is better to spend a day waiting for the wind to die than it is to die yourself (or at least we imagine it is).

4. If you ground a canoe while paddling on a river, jump out on the upstream side. If you don't, your boat might float downstream and hurt you.

5. Water works best outside the canoe. If you take on water, take time to drop it off. A bailing sponge will help here, or the willingness to stop and empty your boat.

6. Keep your weight low. Don't stand up in a canoe without warning everyone else in the boat.

7. Kneeling in the canoe while paddling gives more power, more control, and better stability, so do it in fast water or in bigger-than-average waves.

8. Don't change hands on the paddle or change the side of the canoe on which you are paddling unless you have time to fumble.

9. Communicate with your partner all the time. Don't try to guess what she or he is going to do next.

10. Give a wide berth to snags, rocks, overhangs, tree limbs, bridge piers, docks, and other canoes.

11. Scout rapids before trying to paddle them. If you don't see a clear unobstructed channel, portage around the rapids.

12. Wear a life preserver (PFD) at all times.

A Bit about Water

While all water moves, at least on a molecular level (remember that chemistry course you took in tenth grade?), it is common for canoers to talk about "flatwater," or lakes, as though it is quite still. This makes sense when you compare the motion in lakes to that in rivers—especially in the real fast parts of rivers. Lakes, then, are generally called flatwater, and rivers are moving water. Rapids, the real fast, turbulent parts of rivers, are called whitewater. Beginners should stick to the first two and assiduously avoid the third.

Moving Water

Water is heavy, about a pound per pint. When water is moving, as it does in a current, it has a great deal of inertia. This means that it will try to move in a straight line all the time. Riverbanks, countercurrents from other rivers or channels, and other large obstructions prevent this from happening and turn the water off its line of motion.

Inside curve

In a river, water doesn't turn well until it hits the outside of a bend. Because it turns quickly when it hits a bank, the fastest water follows the outside of the bend. To be safe when you're canoeing around bends, start with the inside of the curve until you're sure the outside is safe.

In fast-moving water, inertia causes the water to flow past large obstacles without filling the space behind them (that is, on the downstream side). The space behind large obstacles, or on the inside of a sharp bend, is, therefore, often filled with

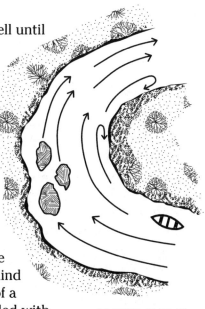

INSIDE CURVE

slack water or by water actually flowing upstream. These "eddies" are good places to pause and rest if you can enter them safely, but they can also be dangerous. If you are trying to leave an eddy, or manage to paddle across one inadvertently, be ready for the twisting force created by the current differential on the edges of the hole.

Eddies

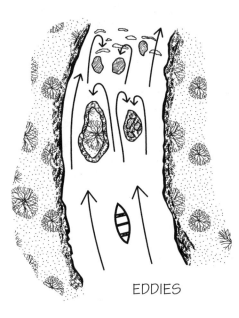

EDDIES

Turbulence is visible downstream of underwater obstructions. If you don't keep this in mind, you are likely to be unpleasantly surprised. Also, large obstructions can create "holes" (see left) that can swamp, and sometimes hold, a canoe and its occupants. Really take care to avoid large obstructions.

You can often see a channel through rapids. Channels are usually defined by a "tongue" or "vee" of slick water followed by "standing waves"—actual waves that just stay in one place. If you are a novice canoer and can't see a clear channel, even on gentle rapids, don't even think about trying to paddle through them. Portages may be painful, but they'll almost never actually kill you. Rapids can!

It is important to remember that, while canoes are designed to move through the water, they also move with it. If you don't make any effort to control your boat, it will move with the current of a river just like a log. It is rarely a good idea for you to just float downstream. When you paddle, the canoe develops its own inertia, and the motion of the canoe makes it possible for the paddlers to control the boat by "fighting" the current. In faster water, you can also control your boat quite effectively by moving more slowly than the water; you manage this by backpaddling. By moving more slowly than the water and by angling your boat across the current, you can get the current to push you. This works so well, that it is possible to "ferry," get pushed by the current, back and forth across a river (at the head of a rapids, for example) without moving downstream at all. This is a nifty skill, and it can really impress the kids, so practice it if you get an opportunity to do so.

Flatwater

When paddling on flatwater, you can often use the wind as you would the current on moving water. You can wind-ferry and/or sail quite effectively on many lakes. It is important to remember, though, that the wind pushes the high points on your canoe, while the current pushes the low ones. The wind can easily cause you to swamp (capsize) if you let it push you too hard. If you do try sailing, never tie two, or more than two, boats together to make a bigger boat. These rafts may be hard to flip, but they're very dangerous if they do.

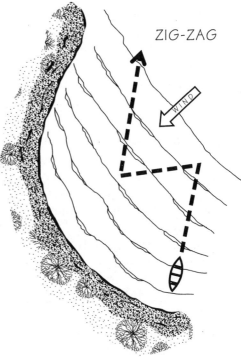

On large lakes, it is usually wise to stay fairly near the shore. Land helps protect you from strong winds, at least if you stay on the upwind shoreline, and provides a refuge in the event of unexpected swims or storms. Staying near shore also gives you more to look at. On the other hand, when paddling near shore you have to be extra alert for underwater snags and hidden obstructions, and for trees and such leaning into your path.

If the lake is wavy, paddle either directly with or directly against the waves (believe it or not, we much prefer the latter) to keep them from breaking over the sides of your canoe. If this doesn't fit your direction of travel, you are better off zigging and zagging your way across a lake than you are trying to paddle in a line perpendicular to the waves.

Canoe Tripping

Almost everything we've said in the preceeding chapters applies to canoe tripping at least as well as it applies to car camping. Some of it may apply even better. There are a few special considerations to keep in mind when planning a canoe trip, and we'll try to get to all of them in some logical order.

Special Equipment

Most 17-foot trip canoes hold about 900 pounds of people and gear, so extra-light equipment isn't a must for canoers, though it helps on those portages, and you don't have to leave a lot of stuff at home. Short canoe trips can, therefore, easily be quite luxurious.

Packing gear in canoes can be a dreadful bore unless you are using duluth packs. Duluth packs are big canvas or nylon sacks with shoulder straps. They are great for canoe trips because they don't have frames or a lot of hooks and buckles on the outside which make for awkward loading, but they do have shoulder straps for carrying the gear from one place to another. Duluth packs come in a bunch of sizes, usually identified by numbers. We generally use numbers 2 or 3 because that's what we're used to and because they're just about the right size for our gear. If, for some reason, you don't have access to duluth packs, duffel bags are a good alternative on trips with no portages because they lack portage carrying capability; and frame packs, even though they're usually too stiff and tall to load easily into a small canoe, will work just fine if you have to portage.

Sleeping bags are important on any camping trip, but because (1) canoeing is a water sport, (2) water gets things wet, (3) people are things, and (4) wet people get cold, bags are really important to canoers. How's that for an irrefutable argument? Down, while it is an exceptionally good insulator, won't work when it's wet, so stick to synthetics for canoeing.

Shoes are important all the time, too, but when we go canoeing,

136

we usually prefer to wear nylon or canvas sneakers. High-tops provide a bit of extra protection, but what you really need to worry about are the soles. Lugged or cleated soles provide almost no traction on slimy, wet rocks, while smooth or ribbed soles, like on a deck shoe, provide a little bit. A little is better than none.

If you are canoeing anywhere out of sight of the car, a map is an essential item, and so is a compass. Getting lost really kills the pleasure on a pleasure trip. Be sure you can read a map before relying on one, though. (See our section on maps in Chapter 6.)

As we've already intimated, a canoe seat can be useful on any trip, but it is really important if you have anyone duffing in your canoe. Sitting on the floor of a boat is fine for an hour or two, but it gets to be a real drag after that. Canoe seats—small, almost leg-less deck chairs built for use in canoes—shouldn't be more than an inch or two above the bottom of the boat or else the weight of the load gets centered too high for safe paddling.

If the bow and stern seats of your canoe aren't padded, a thin piece of closed-cell foam, a sit pad no thicker than about half an inch, will make them much more comfortable. Boat cushions won't work well for canoes because they raise you too high off the seat and can make the boat unstable.

Clothes should all be made of materials that retain some insu-lating ability when wet and that dry easily. On colder days (70° F or less), we almost always paddle in polypropylene, or some simi-lar wicking polyester material, underwear bottoms. It is possible to wear them under wind pants, for modesty's sake. You might miss having pockets if you dress like this, but when you get wet (every time you get into or out of the canoe), you'll like the insu-lating and drying abilities of the polypro/nylon combination.

If you want to be comfortable, you should also have a wind-breaker and rain jacket that are big enough to fit on over your PFD.

Loading a Pack

Because canoeing requires lots of water, and water gets things wet, you should pack your gear in as waterproof a manner as pos-sible. One way to do this is to line your pack with a large plastic garbage bag. If you do this, you have to be careful not to puncture the liner when you pack your gear.

If you don't want to be real careful when packing, or don't like to rely on a single liner, try packing your gear into a number of small stuff sacks, each of which is equipped with its own liner. We typically load our lined duluth packs as described below (from the bottom of the pack, up) and you might want to try it this way, too.

1. Closed-cell foam pad along the bottom of the pack to keep rest of the gear dry and extending up the back to keep sharp edges away from your back when you carry the pack.

2. Trowel, tent poles, and cooking implements (spoon and spatula) in the bottom corners of the pack to fill up otherwise wasted space.

3. Sleeping bag in two stuff sacks with a plastic liner between them (to keep it dry!), packed lengthwise across the bottom of the pack.

4. Pots (in a stuff sack to keep everything else clean) with the lids against the back of the pack for comfort's sake. Your stove might fit inside the pots and your lighter, pliers, bowl, scrubbie, and spoon almost certainly will.

5. Fuel bottles (in brightly colored plastic bags like the ones the Sunday paper sometimes comes in on rainy days) next to the pots.

6. Extra clothes (in a lined stuff sack) next to the fuel bottles.

7. Extra ropes, extra shoes, flashlight, toilet articles (in their own stuff sack), and miscellaneous junk (in yet another small stuff sack) on top of the clothes and pots.

8. Tent and rain fly, in a bag of their own, on top of all this.

9. Food bags (all lined with plastic) on top of the tent.

10. Windbreaker, and anything else you forgot to pack, on top of the food bags.

11. Tarp on top of everything else to help keep it all dry.

In spite of the fact that things can blow away easily, you might want to carry your map and compass (in plastic, of course) on your lap or on the floor of the canoe by your feet. Pack your duct tape, water filter, water bottle, cup, first-aid kit, sunscreen, rain gear, toilet paper (in a plastic bag), and one day's lunch in a day pack, so you can get at them easily. Carry your knife, whistle, and, if you're insecure, a second map in your pants' pockets if you have any. If you hate to lose things, try tying your compass to your shirt, and have the whistle and knife connected to your belt with small pieces of string.

Loading a Canoe

In the interest of clarity, we're going to add a note about caring for your canoe right here, even though there is a section on that later. The note is a simple one: only load your canoe when it's floating in the water. This will probably mean getting your feet wet, but wet feet won't hurt you (not much, anyway), while torn or punctured hulls will.

Most 17-foot canoes come equipped with only two seats: a front and a back. If you haven't figured it out yet, the back seat is the one nearer the end of the canoe. This design feature makes it relatively easy to decide where to load the paddlers. A duffer, as we may have mentioned, should load her or his canoe seat either just in front of, or right behind, the center thwart or portage yoke. If you have two passengers and no gear, one goes in each of the aforementioned spots. Loading just people is easy, and we guess we don't need to say much more about it.

Packing gear into a canoe starts with choosing the right equipment. Work your way through the list we provided earlier and see what you can fit into your packs. Things that don't fit into a pack should be left at home because loose gear gets lost too easily or blows away in a sharp wind. If you need to eliminate something, start with the luxuries and end with the optional equipment. You'll need everything else—except for, perhaps, your pillow.

If you have small bits of gear (cameras, glasses, suntan lotion, water bottles, etc.) that you want to keep easily accessible, pack them in a day pack and carry it under your seat. You should also keep your rain gear near the top of a pack, so you can get it out and on with a minimum of fuss.

If you are planning a trip with lots of portages, keep your load small. It is common, and convenient, to carry three people, two Duluth packs, and one day pack in each canoe. This limits the number of clean shirts you can carry, but it ensures that there is only one pack or one canoe for each person to carry from lake to lake. The person with the canoe also gets the day pack.

Try to keep your canoe on an even keel (or, for the tyro, level in the water). So, assuming your bow and stern paddlers are within 50 pounds of each other, it is best to pack your gear as close to the middle of the boat as possible. If we're carrying a duffer, we load the packs side by side in front of the portage yoke or center thwart, and put the passenger behind it. This keeps the passenger within easy reach so he or she can keep the captain well-fed and happy. If there is no passenger, we pack half our gear in front of the yoke and half behind it. If you are carrying gear, never carry more than one passenger. Most canoes can't handle the weight safely.

When loading packs side by side into the fore or aft compartments of a canoe, try to keep the back straps against the gunwales. This helps prevent the buckles on the front of the pack from getting ripped off accidentally when you pull the packs out. Putting a couple of small sticks, about two inches in diameter, across the floor of the canoe under your packs helps keep them from sitting in a puddle of water all day long.

Care of the Canoe

It is important not to emulate the old pros who like to show off the scars on the bottoms of their boats. Always try to avoid hitting anything in the water, or on the shore, with your canoe. Canoes are not good battering rams and don't stand up well to abuse. Also, you can survive being up the creek without a paddle, but you might not do so well without a canoe.

We already mentioned that you shouldn't load your canoe

unless it is floating in the water. This is also true of unloading it. Putting heavy loads in a boat that is on shore, or even halfway on shore, can bend and sometimes break the hull. You might also puncture the bottom of the boat. Paddling your boat right up to the shore, even onto a sandy beach, is also bad for the bottom— abrasion will damage the hull more slowly, but just as effectively, as hitting a rock head on.

What we're saying here, is that for loading and unloading, wet shoes are the best shoes. Getting in and out of the canoe in a few inches of water won't hurt you, and it might help your canoe live to a ripe old age.

You can generally avoid hitting things by having your bow paddler stay alert. If that isn't possible, or if she or he can't see too clearly, try going real slowly because the force of a collision, if we remember correctly, is equal to mass times velocity. In very murky water, you can even have your bow paddler probe ahead of the canoe for obstacles with the butt of his or her paddle.

Once you have your canoe out of the water for the day, turn it upside down to store it. This lets water drain out of the canoe and helps to protect the hull. It also gives you a dry place (under the canoe) to store surplus gear. When putting a canoe down, try to make sure that the bow, the stern, and the center of one gunwale are actually on the ground. You should also have the hull angled into the wind, so that the wind doesn't get under the boat and blow it away.

If you do manage to broach the hull of your boat, you can probably patch it temporarily with duct tape. You can also try plugging the hole with chewing gum before you tape it. Gum well chewed, packed tightly, and heated with a butane lighter usually makes a pretty solid patch. If you need to patch a hole, tape both sides of the hull.

Caring for your canoe is important, but you also need to be careful with your packs and paddles.

Wood paddles are, generally, the easiest to break. Jamming the tip of the blade into the ground can abrade any varnish away and can split the blade along the grain. If you ignore our advice and use your paddle to push off things, at least use the handle. Plastic paddles are harder to break, but like wood, using them as pry bars or walking sticks can break them. So can stepping on them. Always leave your paddles under the canoe or well away from paths when you aren't using them.

You should always be careful not to overload your packs (if you can't lift them, they're too full), and take care not to lift them off the ground by their straps—doing so often puts too much pressure on the seams and might tear the straps right off of the pack. When lifting a pack, to move it or to put it on, make sure you have solid footing with one foot (for demonstration purposes, the right) slightly in front of the other. Grasp the sides or bottom corners of the pack and lift it to your right knee. Put your right shoulder into the strap and grasp the bottom corner of the pack with your right hand. Swing the pack around your back, put the left strap on, and you're ready to go. If you're lazy, get someone else to lift the pack up for you and have them hang it on your back.

However you lift your pack, remember to keep your back straight and use your leg muscles to do the lifting. Back injuries are incredibly painful.

Portaging

When the lake on which you are paddling ends, or the river gets too wild to handle, you'll need to portage your canoe and gear. This is not surprising, as "a portage" (noun) is a trail between two lakes or around a rapids, and "to portage" (verb) is to carry gear and boats across a portage trail. These definitions may not be exact, but they're sure close enough.

We've already talked about loading and unloading, so we won't say much more now, except to add that you really should unload your canoe before you try to carry it anywhere, otherwise it might break in half.

Once your canoe is unloaded at a portage trail head, you have three options: reload and go home, carry the canoe across the trail, or get someone to carry the boat for you. The first option is no fun—what are you out here for, anyway? And few of us can afford the third, so let's go with the second.

There are a couple of right ways to carry your canoe. The easiest over short, generally open and unobstructed distances is to have one person at each end (ideally on opposite sides of the boat) grasp a gunwale. We say gunwale now, and we do mean it. If you grab the decks, they might just tear right off the canoe. It isn't likely that this will happen, but it is possible, and it would be just awful if it did, so don't let it. If both your lifters lift the canoe by the gunwales and walk slowly, you'll find your canoe moving. Over longer distances, or on portage trails where maneuverability is important, it's a good idea to use the portage yoke.

The best and safest way, as far as we're concerned, to pick up a canoe to portage is easier to demonstrate than to explain, but we'll try to explain it anyway. To portage a canoe with the yoke, follow these steps in order.

1. Unload the canoe and remove it from the water.

2. Put the canoe down, gently, on the ground, on its hull.

3. Get two people to help and all stand facing the canoe:
    a. the first helper at the front thwart;
    b. you (the canoe carrier/portager) at the portage yoke;
    c. the second helper at the back thwart.

4. Plant your feet firmly on the ground, spread apart to about shoulder width and pointed toward the canoe. Have your helpers do the same thing.

5. All three people grasp the near gunwale with both hands and lift the boat to about knee height.

6. All three of you sit back a little with your knees bent so your thighs are at about a 40-degree angle to your shins. The canoe's hull should now be resting on your knees (or, even better, on the "table" made by your thighs).

7. Identify the hand (actually hands) that is (are) on the bow end of the boat.

8. Reach across the boat with your bow hands and grasp the far gunwale with your thumbs inside the canoe. If you can't reach all the way across the canoe, grab as

far out on the thwart or yoke as you can reach and
hold it tightly.

9. Pull the far gunwale towards you, while pushing the
   near one away. This should turn the canoe so that it is
   resting on your "table" on its gunwale, with the hull
   pointed away from your bodies.

10. Make sure the thumb on your stern hand, which is on
    the bottom gunwale, is inside the boat. Grasp the top
    gunwale with your bow hand, if you haven't already
    done so, with your thumb in.

11. Without moving your feet, lift the canoe above your
    heads. It helps to rock it gently and lift it on a
    three-count.

12. Lower the canoe onto the portager's shoulders, with
    the yoke running behind his or her head. Try to
    portage a canoe with the yoke across your throat and
    you'll wonder why it's so hard to breathe.

The portager should carry the canoe pretty much parallel to
the ground, with her or his arms extended forward, and his or her
hands gripping the gunwale with thumbs outside the boat, and fingers inside—this is to prevent the fingers from catching on tree
limbs and breaking off. The others present should grab the packs,
paddles, and PFDs and follow the canoe closely.

When the canoe carrier gets tired (anywhere from a few feet to
a few hundred yards into the portage), she or he can rest one of
three ways.

A "pose" is a tree limb or post about six or seven or more feet
off the ground in a clear spot next to the portage trail. By lifting
the bow of the canoe, walking up to the pose, carefully placing the
stern on the ground, and just as carefully placing the gunwales of
the canoe on this piece of wood, a canoe carrier can get a lot of
weight off her or his shoulders. Unfortunately, poses are almost
never there when you need them (unless, of course, you built the
trail yourself and knew exactly how far you could carry your canoe).

If a pose isn't handy but a pack carrier is, you can "bridge" the boat. The packer should drop (figuratively—put packs down gently every time) his or her load while the canoe carrier places the stern gently on the ground. The packer, now the "bridge," can then stand under the canoe, in front of and facing, the canoe carrier. After planting her feet firmly, the bridge should grasp the gunwales of the boat and lift it above her head until her arms are straight. If the boat is heavy, the canoe carrier might need to help with this step. If a third person is present, he should drop (again, figuratively) his pack, and take over the role of canoe carrier. You can then continue the portage until it is time to switch roles again.

The third acceptable way to rest should be obvious. Work through the same steps you went through to pick up the canoe in reverse and put it down. You should get as far to the side of the trail as possible if you elect this option, so other portagers don't trip over you.

A fourth way to rest is to throw the canoe to the ground, and a fifth is to collapse under it, but these don't really work so well, so avoid them.

Choosing a Campsite

If you are canoeing anywhere in the U.S.A., you will almost certainly be required, or at least strongly encouraged, to camp only in designated campsites. This is a good thing to do, as it limits your impact and allows you to have a cooking fire if you want one. Most designated sites are also equipped with a pit toilet, which can be convenient.

Sometimes, in other countries (like, say, Canada—in the Quetico Provincial Park), and even in some places in the U.S., you can camp anywhere you want as long as it isn't private property or the middle of a trail. In this case, pick an established or designated campsite anyway. It is important not to harden more sites than are already hardened.

A campsite for canoeing should be well shielded from the lake or river and shouldn't have any dead trees hanging over the flat spot where you plan to put your tent. Dead trees can fall in the night, or even in the day, and you never want to be under one when that happens.

Chapter 8

One Step Farther
Hiking & Backpacking

Canoeing is an easy way to get into the backcountry because there are lakes and rivers all over the place and because canoeing doesn't require much specialized equipment. It's also fun because you can carry almost as much as you want. Not everyone is into canoeing, though, and even those of you who are, might get bored with it year after year. One way to see the backcountry sans canoe and sans car is to pack in. This is not quite as simple as canoeing because you are limited to what you can carry at one time, but it can be just as rewarding. If nothing else, it is worth thinking about. That said, we'll keep our word and offer a few hundred words about being a pack mule.

A Bit about Backpacking

The first thing you have to keep in mind when you consider backpacking is that you can't carry as much as your average car, or even your average canoe. A car will hold upwards of 300 pounds of gear per passenger (that's a guess, not a scientifically established figure), and a canoe will hold, maybe not easily, 150 pounds per person (assuming three people averaging 150 pounds each and a 900-pound maximum capacity in the boat). A back-pack, on the other hand, usually limits you to gear weighing no more than one-third to one-half your body weight, assuming you are a reasonably fit and healthy individual. On a good day, when we're feeling very fit, either of us can carry more than that, but we have years of experience working on our side. Even so, neither of us will ever try to pack more than 70 or 80 pounds for more than a few yards at a time.

As a rule, 40 to 60 pounds is a reasonable average weight for a fully loaded pack for healthy adult packers. Packs can't be too light if they are holding everything you need, so never, ever let reason and average rules tell you you aren't carrying enough weight to have fun. How much you carry probably should be limited on the upper end by the one-half body weight rule, but the final determination has to be how comfortable you are with a loaded pack on your back. If packs are too heavy, packing is no fun.

Backpacks

Internal Frame

External Frame

Before you can even think about going on a backpacking trip, you have to locate a good pack. Come to think of it, if you didn't think about it first, you'd have no need to locate a pack, so go ahead and think. (Who are we to shatter your dreams?) But, do promise you won't do anything about your thoughts before you locate the pack.

In an earlier section we talked a bit about the two most common types of packs suitable for backpacking: internal frame packs and external frame packs. You might want to review that section now. While either of these two types of packs, or any of the newer hybrids, will work for most beginners' trips, external-frame packs generally hold more weight comfortably than their internally framed counterparts, and they also tend to be less expensive ($80 and up for a reasonable external frame and about twice that for a reasonable internal frame). Both sorts are also fairly easy to rent. Given the cost considerations, we usually recommend beginners start with an external-frame pack (from Camp Trails, Kelty, EMS, REI, or somewhere else).

Packs—this discussion covers only external frames from here on out—come in all sorts of sizes and shapes, are constructed from all sorts of materials, and have all sorts of design features unique to the manufacturer. In general, a good frame pack will have a solidly built aluminum frame with a slight "S" shape to it, a pair of sturdy padded shoulder straps (contoured or curved ones are generally more comfortable than straight ones), a padded hip belt and webbed back band, and a pack cloth or nylon bag attached to the frame.

We could go on and on here about details of design, construction, and fashion relating to backpacks, but we really don't think that's necessary. For short trips, almost any solidly built frame pack will work just fine, even a rented one, and this section is only about short-trip camping. You do have to consider a couple of features carefully, though.

The bag of the pack will usually be about two-thirds as long as the frame, leaving space on the bottom to tie on a sleeping bag, and it should have a capacity of from 2000 to 4000 cubic inches. If you are strong, and like to carry a lot of stuff, you'll probably prefer a bigger bag. We do, however, know a lot of people who figure smaller is better because then they aren't tempted to try to carry too much.

Pack frames come in different sizes for different sized backs. Labels, you will find, are based on average back lengths, and averages don't fit individuals. A pack labeled: "Large—fits from 5'6" to 6'," might actually fit everyone from five and a half to six feet tall, but that isn't likely. One of us is barely six feet but needs an extra-large frame, and we have a five-foot, four-inch friend who needs a large, instead of the medium the manufacturer recommends. The only way to make sure a pack fits is to try it on when it is loaded with as much weight as you'll be carrying on the trail. Good stores keep sand bags on hand so this is easy to do. Make sure your pack fits comfortably before you take it on a trip, and find out how to adjust the fit, just in case things change.

Shoes & Boots

We mentioned in an earlier chapter that you should always take two pairs of shoes camping with you. One pair, usually smooth-soled sneakers, is for evening wear, and one pair is for daytime wear. If you're backpacking with a heavy load, your day-time shoes should probably be light- or medium-weight boots. If you don't have a heavy load (if you're just on a one- or two-day trip), stiff-soled running shoes might be just as good.

Heavy technical mountaineering boots (the kind they always wear in the mountain-climbing pictures) are environmentally destructive and so heavy that you'll be sick of walking before you get out of the parking lot. For most hiking, lightweight leather, or nylon-and-leather, boots are more than adequate, providing they have good soles and provide substantial support for your arches.

If you are going to be walking on rough surfaces or unpaved trails and want to be comfortable crossing small streams and boulder fields, a lugged sole (like Vibram™ makes) is still your best bet. As we said earlier, though, on smoother surfaces and paved trails, any reasonably stiff, rough sole, like those on decent running shoes, should suffice to keep you moving in the direction you want to go. A stiff sole is important when you're wearing a pack, because it will help prevent bruises on the bottoms of your feet.

Selecting Your Gear

Because the amount of gear you can carry is limited by its total weight, it is nice to have some specialized equipment when you go backpacking. Ultra-expensive, ultra-light equipment isn't really necessary for short (one- or two- or three-night) trips. Decent car camping equipment may weigh a bit more than is necessary, but it should be just fine for packing.

As with canoe trips, a good way to meet your equipment needs is to work through the equipment list (a modified list is provided below) from the beginning, making sure you keep all the essentials

—food for as many days as you are planning to be out, clothes, cooking stuff, water, sunscreen, and stuff like that. Once you have everything essential together, weigh it, and—if you're lucky—add anything else you want up to your maximum weight load. If you find that your essential equipment exceeds your maximum weight, start trimming off labels and excess packaging until you lose enough, or consider taking a burly friend along on your trip.

Basic Equipment for Backpacking
(moderate weather only)

Group Equipment (1–4 people)

stove (1 burner)
$1^{1}/2$ - & 1-qt. pots, frying pan, lids
pliers or pot gripper
spoon & spatula
nylon pot scrubber
water filter
food (3 meals/person/day)
garbage bag
trowel
toilet paper
candle lantern
insect repellent
biodegradable soap

toothpaste
$^{1}/2$ qt. of fuel/day, pour spout for fuel
coffee pot & lid
lighter &/or matches
water bladder
2 @ 50' light nylon ropes
tarp (waterproof)
tents/s, tent poles & aluminum stakes
repair kit
extra candles
sunscreen
hand lotion
extra map

Individual Equipment

emergency food & shelter
sleeping pad
map/s, compass
small pocket knife
cup, bowl, spoon
flashlight
lighter

first-aid kit
sleeping bag & stuff sack
whistle
water bottle
sunglasses
day pack (optional)
bear bell (optional)

toilet articles (large bandana, toothbrush, lip balm, tampons, small supply of toilet paper)

Individual Clothes (to wear & carry)

hat with brim	wool hat
2 pair underwear	2 T-shirts
long johns (tops & bottoms)	4 pairs of wool socks
gloves or mittens	1 pair shorts
long wool or bunting pants	long-sleeved wool or bunting shirt
down vest or extra wool shirt	sneakers
boots	gaiters
raincoat & pants	wind coat & pants

Optional Equipment

books	field guides
fishing gear	camera & film
cards and/or games	walking stick
harmonica	thermometer
diary & pencil	binoculars
sit pads	watch

This equipment list is a general guide, not an absolute one. In dry areas, for example, you need to carry all your own water—four or five quarts/person/day at a weight of about two pounds/quart. Generally, this list should prove sufficient for trips from two to ten days. Trips longer than about ten days require food drops, and you shouldn't even consider them at this point in your packing career.

You may have noticed that this equipment list is a bit more sparse than the earlier one. There is, of course, a weighty reason for that.

While backpacking can teach you a lot about what you can do without, there are two, actually, three, things you can't do without. These are food and water, and shelter. Because you want to carry lots of food—packing takes energy—and you might have to carry all your own water (sometimes necessary in the desert), you want to carry as light a shelter as possible. Limiting extra clothes to a bare minimum can help, as can avoiding huge tents of any material, any tents made of canvas, and all those ultra-heavy cotton-batting sleeping bags. So, stick with the lightweight stuff we discussed earlier.

Notes about Equipment

The most important piece of equipment you can carry with you anywhere is a good attitude. You'll have to make sure you remember to put that in your pocket before you leave the house. Unfortunately, a good attitude, while valuable, is not sufficient without the right equipment.

While most good car-camping equipment is adequate for backpacking, we would like to clarify what we mean by "good." If your car-camping experience has proved, beyond any reasonable doubt, that your equipment is warm and durable enough for life in the out-of-doors, then it might be good. If, on the other hand, you haven't ever managed to sleep out without turning on the heater and your clothes self-destruct every time you get more than ten miles from downtown, then your equipment probably isn't good.

Packing a Pack

Frame packs can be loaded lots of different ways, and everyone likes to load theirs a bit differently. Most experts develop systems for packing, so they know where every piece of equipment is. Our favorite system is called the garbage can, and we're never sure where anything we don't really need is packed.

Start by tying your sleeping bag, and any clothes you can fit in the stuff sack with your bag, to the bottom of the pack frame. Use nylon parachute cord to tie the bag on, rather than elastic "bungee" cords, because rope is more secure and the load bounces less.

Shove your extra shoes, extra clothes, and lightweight junk into the bottom compartment and pack your heaviest stuff at the bottom of the top compartment (just above the middle of the pack, going from bottom to top). Your water bottle, fuel bottle, and first-aid kit go in the side pockets of the pack, and your sleeping pad, day pack, tent poles, and rain gear get tied onto the top of the frame. Lunch usually goes in your pockets or on the very top of the pack, so you can nibble all day long without digging. Everything else goes anywhere it fits. It is a good idea to keep the weight centered in the top third of the pack, as close to your back as possible, but other than that, how you load is a personal matter.

If you pack in this highly organized manner, you might like to unpack by getting your food out of the pack and into the kitchen, setting up a tent, and dumping the rest of your gear from your pack into it. That way you won't lose small stuff in the grass or under rocks.

Lifting a Pack

We discussed picking up a pack in the last chapter, but we think it's important to mention it again here. Whenever you are lifting a pack you should make sure you have solid footing and do your lifting with your thigh muscles, not your lower back. This is usually accomplished by squatting down with your back straight, grasping the pack tightly, and standing up. To put a pack on without tearing the shoulder straps off the frame:

1. Stand facing the frame side of the pack with your right foot slightly in front of the left.

2. Grasp the sides or bottom corners of the pack, and lift it to your right knee.

3. Put your right arm and shoulder into the right strap, and grasp the bottom (right) corner of the pack with your right hand.

4. (You can reach around your back with your left hand, if you want, to help guide this step.) Swing the pack around your back and put the left strap on.

5. Cinch your hip belt, adjust your shoulder straps, and connect anything else that needs connecting (maybe a chest strap). This should leave you ready to go.

If you are generally lazy, and have a helper handy, get her or him to lift the pack up for you and step backwards into the straps.

Safety

Backpacking can be a fun solo sport, but beginners should always make it a group effort. You can solo after you've got about 50 years of experience. Other safety tips aren't overly complicated.

1. Know where you are at all times. Check your map against markers on the trail or against natural features (lakes, ridges, etc.) to insure that you don't get lost.

2. Everyone in the group should have a map and compass and know how to use them, and everyone should know where they are and where they are going.

3. Don't hike faster than the slowest member of your group. Groups that don't stick together aren't groups at all.

4. Hike on trails where they exist. Trying to cut cross-country rarely saves time, but it usually increases your chances of getting lost, and it always increases your impact on the environment.

5. If the trail is wet and muddy, stay on it anyway, but be careful not to slip and fall. Walking next to a muddy trail will eventually result in two parallel muddy trails, and you shouldn't contribute to that type of parallelism.

6. If you have to cross small streams or large puddles without the assistance of bridges (Lloyd, Beau, or suspension), walk slowly right on through the water. Your feet will dry, and keeping them from getting wet isn't worth risking a fall.

7. Take a couple of minutes to wring out your socks and air your feet after walking through the water. This might help prevent blisters (we've never really noticed that it does) and will certainly help protect that positive attitude.

8. Treat blisters before they become a problem. Two pairs

of socks inside your boots and the immediate application of moleskin to "hot-spots," warm, inflamed spots where you are about to get a blister, will generally prevent them from becoming a problem.

9. Hiking should be fun, so don't wear yourself out. Go slowly, take frequent breaks, and stop to smell (or photograph) the roses. Go for quality miles not quantity.

10. Don't ever count on catching fish for dinner. Carry enough food for as many days as you'll be on the trail. If you don't eat everything, that's fine; you can take it home and save it for the next trip.

11. Eat and drink (water, of course) often, throughout the day.

In the Mountains

One of the pieces of conventional wisdom related to mountain hiking is to "hike high and camp low." Keep this in mind when you head for the hills. High-altitude hiking is a joy, especially if you can get above the tree line—you get to see for miles (which is thrilling and often makes navigating easier), there are relatively few obstructions, and the reduced oxygen makes for an easily obtainable "runner's high." Camping at lower elevations usually gives you better access to water which, of course, flows downhill and pools in lower places, and provides for easier, more sheltered, and more comfortable sleeping.

To be on the safe side, we usually recommend that beginners stay on marked trails and avoid the perils of scree fields (loose gravel on the sides of mountains), glaciers (which can have thinly covered crevasses into which the unwary might fall), and dangerously narrow ledges high above the ground. Trails tend to take you around these dangers and can be thrilling enough on their own.

Pretty much everything we've mentioned in other sections of this book applies to the mountains, too. You still have to be careful, you still have to pay attention to where you're going, and you should still have fun. The only real hazards peculiar to the mountains are an increased likelihood of dangerous falls (which is covered under "be careful") and altitude-related illnesses (which are discussed later in this chapter).

Shade

The sun gets real bright when you're up high, so shade, for your head and your eyes, is really important. Wear a hat with a wide brim and good sunglasses when you're in the mountains.

Glasses should block at least 90 percent of the harmful UV rays; good ones will block 97 percent or more. The lenses should be gray if you want to see colors the way you would without glasses, but can be rose colored or green if you like to see the world in a different light.

Capping Peaks

One of the things you get to do in the mountains that you can't do anywhere else is capping peaks. Climbing to the very top of a mountain is, for many hikers, the ultimate thrill, and if you ever do it, you'll probably understand why. We do it so we can say we did, and so we get to write our names in the log book that is often placed in a cairn of stones on the mountain top. (Sometimes it's actually a log slip-of-paper in a film canister.)

If you do hike in the mountains, we would caution you against focusing all your aspirations on capping peaks. Sometimes the difficulty of the terrain makes it unlikely, and more often the weather makes it impossible. If climbing to the "top" is your only goal, not making it can ruin a trip. Peaks should only be a part of the experience—gravy, so to speak, on your mashed potatoes (which, unlike potato, does have an "e")—and the hike should be just as fun without them.

Altitude-related Illnesses

If you live way up in the mountains, you probably don't have to give a lot of thought to the effects of altitude on your body. If, however, you live in the flatlands, there are a few things you need to be aware of.

Above about 5,000 feet (that is, towards the clouds from Denver), altitude sickness or acute mountain sickness can be a problem, particularly if you are a low-lander and ascend rapidly, as you do in a car. Anyone can suffer from the effects of altitude—even young, healthy climbers—so be careful.

Generally, altitude problems can be prevented by taking time to acclimatize yourself to new altitudes. Start your mountain trip at a lower elevation, say 5,000 feet or so, and relax (sit around, read, rest, rest, rest) for your first day or two until your body gets used to lower oxygen levels. Then you can move slowly, on foot, up to higher elevations.

Early symptoms of altitude sickness are similar to the symptoms of exhaustion and include pain (headaches, muscle aches), dizziness, uneasy sleep, difficulty breathing, rapid pulse rates, nausea or vomiting, and symptoms of dehydration. If you experience these symptoms, it is important to rest, drink plenty of fluids, breath deeply, and (usually) move to a lower altitude to camp. If symptoms persist, or begin to get worse, rest more often (every step or two, if necessary) and keep moving down the mountain.

More serious altitude-related conditions include pulmonary and cerebral edema. These are very serious and require medical treatment.

Pulmonary edema, a pooling of fluids in the lungs, has symptoms resembling pneumonia: difficulty breathing, persistent coughing, wheezing, and the symptoms of altitude sickness. Cerebral edema, a swelling of the brain, is indicated by confusion, poor balance, and lethargy. If you notice these symptoms, move immediately to a lower altitude and seek medical attention. A failure to treat these condition quickly can prove fatal, so it is best to assume, until a qualified doctor says otherwise, that any condition that might be an edema is one.

A camper suffering from an altitude-related illness will almost certainly be unable to carry equipment and may need to be assisted or carried down the mountain. If the need arises, carry the sick camper to a lower elevation first and ferry the equipment down later.

Other Comments on the Sport

Hiking should be fun, so relax and enjoy it. Walk slowly, place your feet carefully, keep your balance at all times (never try jumping with a pack on your back), and you shouldn't have any real problems.

If you are destination oriented—that is, if the reason you are hiking is to get to a particular place for a camping trip, try to enjoy the hike there and back anyway. Once you are at your destination, think about day hikes to other secluded spots. Walking is great exercise, and it is also a wonderful way to see the world.

Both of us are always astounded, whenever we get into a car after camping for a few days, at how little we can see when we're moving at 30 or 40 or 60 miles an hour. Walking along at a paltry 3 or 4 miles an hour (or 1 mph with a heavy pack) we're always amazed by how very colorful and alive the world is. It's hard to get that feeling in the city—especially if you're in a hurry—so take advantage of it while you're on the trail.

photo by Norm Kerr

Chapter 9

The Real Stuff?
Using What You've Learned

You've read and learned all about the philosophy and techniques of minimum impact camping, you've invested in a high quantity of high-quality, yet reasonably priced, camping gear, you're primed for action, hot-to-(fox?)-trot, ready to hit the hills, and all sorts of stuff like that, so how do you actually find a place to go camping? Well, that, dear reader, is entirely up to you.

There are a number of good ways to find a camping place. One way is to call your home state's (or any state's or province's, as far as that goes) Office of Tourism, a regional business association, or the Chamber of Commerce in an area known for camping, ask for a listing of available campgrounds, read it, and then go to one. Another way is to look for an interesting state or national park (you can check the library for a guide book or call the Park Service) and go there. You could also just bop out to your own backyard. If you've never camped before, we'd suggest you start out with a backyard—preferably your own, but a neighbor's will do—or a state park, because they are generally the easiest to find and feel safer than many other places.

A number of these parks are also designed, or at least their facilities are, to be accessible to people with disabilities. While not everyone with a disability needs specialized facilities—it would be an insult to think that this is so—even a lot of people not in wheelchairs appreciate solid trails with minimal grades, wide stalls in outhouses, and other modifications intended to make areas more accessible.

Before you go anywhere, make sure you secure all the necessary permits, and always make reservations, if you can, between the special and popular months of May through September, when the days dwindle down to a precious few as far as most campers are concerned. The parks do fill up fast, especially on holiday weekends, and getting to the campground and finding that it's full can spoil your fun real fast.

Once you locate a campground, reserve a site, secure permits, plan your trip, prepare your equipment, load the car, drive to the campground, unpack everything, and set up camp, you can do most anything you want. When the camp is set up and the coffee is brewing, the work ends and the fun starts.

We honestly think (can we think dishonestly?) the most important activity associated with camping in which you can participate is concentrating on being alive. You might also search for a modicum of self-awareness. The world really is alive, and we all are a part of that life. Stopping whatever it is we usually do for a little while to be a part of the world can make us all better people. If you don't go for this contemplative stuff, you might prefer going for a long walk along a scenic trail, looking for birds or insects, reading a good book (try Walton's *The Compleat Angler*), fishing, or just "hanging out." All of those can be part of being alive, too, with or without the contemplation.

No matter what else you do, sleep under the moon and stars, without a tent over your head at least once, just so you know what it's like. You won't believe how many stars there are that won't show themselves near the city lights and how different the sounds of the night can be when they're not muffled by walls, even the thin ones of a tent. If sleeping under the moon and stars wasn't so great, we never would have used it as a chapter title.

Free Choice and Positive Attitudes

Camping allows a lot of personal freedom because it isn't necessary for everyone to "camp" in exactly the same way. What we consider a great time might be a real drag for you, and vice versa, but as long as we don't interfere with each other's experience, and as long as we both practice minimum impact techniques, it does not matter at all if we don't do the same things. That's because camping isn't really any particular activity.

We admit that sleeping in a sleeping bag and cooking in a battered pot over a minute little stove are often part of the camping experience, but they certainly aren't the activities that define "camping" for us. Such a wide range of individual choices are potentially, and legitimately, a part of camping, that the actual activities (within reason and the constraints of minimum impact philosophy) seem to us to be less important than the spirit in which they are done. That's why we say that camping is an attitude, rather than an activity.

We really love being in the outdoors. While we would prefer it if everyone else stayed away from *our* favorite places, we want everyone else to love the outdoors as much as we do. We also believe that everyone can. All it takes is the right attitude. We're not saying that everyone will love rugged, backcountry camping. That simply isn't true. But we are saying that some form of camping can be fun for everyone if they'll let it be fun, and if they don't expect it to be something it can't be.

Camping will be different from home. Living outdoors means you live with what the outdoors holds: if it rains, you get rained on; if there are mosquitoes, they will bite you; and if the temperature drops, you can't turn on the heat. Sometimes camping is hard work, but it is often worth it. At home, you can't often catch a fish before breakfast, look through the window at a browsing moose, or see the alpine glow against the backdrop of an undeveloped mountain ridge. Few backyards provide the sights or sounds or smells of a wild pine forest, and even fewer allow the solitude and grandeur of a pristine wilderness.

Camping can be "roughing it," but it certainly doesn't have to be. We can say, quite honestly, that we are as comfortable camping as we are at home, even if we are a little dirtier.

Once upon a time, just to give you an example, we were backpacking in the mountains a bit east of Yellowstone Park. We hiked into the wilds at a leisurely pace over the course of several days and set up camp in a sheltered valley on the edge of an alpine meadow. Our site overlooked one of the most beautiful lakes in the world and provided a panoramic view of the mountains. Once we were set up for the night, we were able to settle into lounge chairs made up of sleeping pads and conveniently located boulders, pour ourselves a drink of tea, and watch a herd of mountain goats graze their way across the meadow. Both the plot and the action were more interesting than most of the shows on television.

What we're saying here, to be sure you get the point, is that the clothes and equipment we carry really do make camping much more comfortable than many people would believe. And our expectations and attitude make camping a joy in spite of the weather, insects, and work.

We do know a few people who won't agree with us on this one—too much dirt and too little electricity make anything approaching comfort impossible for some folks—but almost everyone we've ever taken camping has managed to adjust their attitude enough that they had a good time.

We hope that you can too.

A Last Philosophical Note

We can't pretend that our advocacy of environmental preservation and minimum impact camping techniques doesn't ever come into conflict with our recommendation that you use equipment manufactured from refined metals and man-made, mostly petrochemical-based, materials. It does. If we really wanted to "minimize" our impact on the environment, we would only use natural fibers and eat organic foods that were gathered and prepared nonviolently. You might want to live that way, but we really don't.

People—all of us—are a natural part of the environment, and not all of the changes we introduce into the environment are necessarily negative ones. Beavers dam creeks, birds build nests, badgers dig burrows, and people process materials. It is not wrong for us to use resources that the "natural" or nonhuman environment provides. It is wrong, though, for us to destroy the environment in pursuit of those resources or in pursuit of a few hours of recreation.

Camping in undeveloped, minimally damaged reserves can let us see a better world. The few "wild," or minimally affected, areas left in North America can help remind us of how wonderful our planet was in the past, and they might also be patterns for the future. Camping in these areas can let us practice a simple, less consumptive lifestyle, and more importantly, it can bring us into close physical and emotional contact with life. Camping can help us see that it is important to preserve the environment for our own sakes and for the sake of the environment itself. Because of this, a belief in preservation, or at least conservation, and camping are inseparable. If you don't believe that, you have no business in the outdoors, and we—as individuals and as a species—have little hope for the future.

Camping is a pleasure, but every pleasure carries with it some responsibility. The responsibility campers have is to care for this planet as well as themselves. So, whether you camp, or you just think about camping, be a good camper—take care of yourself, and take care of your home, too.

Appendix

Checklists, Sample Menu, & Answers to the Minimum
Impact Quiz

I. Planning Checklist

Advance Planning

☐ permits secured

☐ reservations made and confirmed

☐ directions to campground clearly understood

☐ maps of area secured

Before Leaving Home

☐ informed someone of plans & return date

☐ equipment checked

☐ equipment packed

☐ clothes checked

☐ clothes packed

☐ food checked

☐ food packed

☐ first-aid kit checked

☐ first-aid kit packed

☐ car loaded

II. Basic Equipment Checklist
Ready to go Camping

Group Equipment
Kitchen Equipment

- ☐ stove/s
- ☐ fuel for stove/s
- ☐ pour spout or funnel for fuel
- ☐ 2-qt. & 1-qt. pots with lids (minimum list)
- ☐ coffee pot & lid
- ☐ frying pan & lid
- ☐ pliers or pot gripper
- ☐ mixing spoon & spatula
- ☐ lighter &/or matches
- ☐ water filter
- ☐ water bladder or jug

- ☐ food bags
- ☐ food (enough for 3 meals/person/day)
- ☐ 50'–100' light nylon rope
- ☐ 100'–200' parachute cord
- ☐ garbage bag
- ☐ tarp (waterproof)
- ☐ pot scrubber (nylon)
- ☐ tongs (optional)
- ☐ grate (only for cooking on a fire)
- ☐ towel/s
- ☐ spice kit

Campsite Equipment

- ☐ tarp (waterproof)
- ☐ trowel
- ☐ tent/s
- ☐ tent poles
- ☐ tent stakes
- ☐ first-aid kit (group)

- ☐ repair kit (for tent, clothes, stove, etc.)
- ☐ toilet paper
- ☐ candle lantern
- ☐ extra candles
- ☐ emergency food & shelter

Individual Equipment
Personal Equipment

- ☐ closed-cell foam pad
- ☐ sleeping bag (and stuff sack)
- ☐ pillow
- ☐ map/s
- ☐ compass
- ☐ whistle
- ☐ small pocket knife water bottle

- ☐ cup, bowl, spoon, knife, fork, plate
- ☐ towel or large bandana
- ☐ toothbrush & paste
- ☐ lip balm
- ☐ biodegradable soap
- ☐ tampons or sanitary napkins

- ☐ hand lotion
- ☐ sunglasses
- ☐ sunscreen
- ☐ flashlight (extra batteries)
- ☐ day pack
- ☐ insect repellent
- ☐ sit pad

168

Personal Luxury Items

☐ small folding chair ☐ hammock
☐ solar shower ☐ books

Accessories & Optional Equipment

☐ camera & film ☐ diary & pencil
☐ fishing gear ☐ note book
☐ cards ☐ binoculars
☐ games ☐ watch
☐ harmonica/guitar ☐ thermometer
☐ toys ☐ more books
☐ walking stick ☐ field guides (birds, insects, plants, mammals)
☐ bear bell

Clothing

Head Wear

☐ hat with brim
☐ wool stocking cap

First Layer

☐ 2 pair underwear ☐ wool gloves
☐ 2 T-shirts ☐ cotton work gloves
☐ long underwear tops & bottoms ☐ optional other
☐ 3 or 4 pairs of wool socks

Second Layer

☐ 1 pair shorts ☐ 1 pair of light- to medium-weight
☐ 1 pair long wool or fleece pants ☐ boots (or second pair of sneakers)
☐ 1 long-sleeved wool or fleece shirt ☐ chamois shirt
☐ 1 lightweight down vest or second ☐ chinos
  wool shirt ☐ optional other
☐ 1 pair sneakers or moccasins

Last Layer

☐ raincoat	☐ wind pants
☐ rain pants	☐ optional other
☐ windbreaker	☐ bandanas 3–12 in various colors

III. Basic First-Aid Equipment Checklist

Personal First-Aid Kit

☐ anti-inflammatory (aspirin or ibuprofen)

☐ analgesic (acetaminophen)

☐ antacid

☐ adhesive bandage strips (various shapes & sizes for minor cuts & scrapes)

☐ moleskin or mole foam (for blisters)

☐ antihistamine (for minor allergic reactions)

☐ tweezers (for slivers)

☐ roller gauze (2 @ 2" x 5 yards)

☐ safety pins (several)

☐ sterile gauze pads (at least 4 @ 4" x 4")

☐ sanitary napkin (as bulk dressing for severe bleeding)

☐ cloth tape (2" wide x 30')

☐ triangle bandage

☐ elastic bandages (2" ankle wrap & 4" knee wrap)

☐ thermometer

☐ 2 quarters & list of emergency numbers (for phone calls)

☐ anti-bacterial soap

☐ calamine lotion

☐ oval eye pad

☐ anti-fungal ointment

☐ anti-bacterial ointment

☐ personal medications

☐ extra map & compass (for emergency use)

IV. Canoe Camping Checklist
(2–8 people)

Specialized Equipment

☐ canoes (1 every 2-3 people)

☐ paddles (3/canoe)

☐ PFDs (1/person)

☐ duluth packs or duffel bags (2-3/canoe)

170

Kitchen Equipment—Group

- ☐ stove/s (2 one-burner models)
- ☐ fuel for stove/s (1 qt/day)
- ☐ pour spout or funnel for fuel
- ☐ 2-qt. & 1-qt. pots with lids
- ☐ coffee pot & lid
- ☐ frying pan & lid
- ☐ pliers or pot gripper
- ☐ mixing spoon & spatula
- ☐ lighter &/or matches
- ☐ water filter
- ☐ water bladder or jug
- ☐ food bags
- ☐ food (enough for 3 meals/person/day)
- ☐ 50'–100' lightweight nylon rope
- ☐ 100'–200' parachute cord
- ☐ garbage bag
- ☐ tarp (waterproof)
- ☐ pot scrubber (nylon)
- ☐ tongs (optional)
- ☐ grate (only for cooking on a fire)
- ☐ towel/s
- ☐ spice kit

Campsite Equipment–Group

- ☐ tarp (waterproof)
- ☐ trowel
- ☐ tent/s, poles, & stakes
- ☐ first-aid kit (group)
- ☐ repair kit (for tent, clothes, stove, etc.)
- ☐ toilet paper
- ☐ candle lantern
- ☐ extra candles
- ☐ emergency food & shelter

Personal Equipment—Individual

- ☐ closed-cell foam pad (for sleeping)
- ☐ sleeping bag (and stuff sack)
- ☐ pillow
- ☐ map/s
- ☐ compass
- ☐ whistle
- ☐ small pocket knife (adults only)
- ☐ water bottle
- ☐ cup, bowl, spoon, knife, fork, plate
- ☐ towel or large bandana
- ☐ toothbrush & paste
- ☐ lip balm
- ☐ biodegradable soap
- ☐ tampons or sanitary napkins
- ☐ hand lotion
- ☐ sunglasses
- ☐ sunscreen
- ☐ flashlight & extra batteries
- ☐ day pack
- ☐ insect repellent
- ☐ "wet" shoes

Luxury Items & Optional Equipment—Individual or Group

- [ ] canoe seats
- [ ] solar shower
- [ ] hammock/s
- [ ] books
- [ ] fishing gear
- [ ] camera & film
- [ ] more books
- [ ] cards, games, cribbage board
- [ ] harmonica or other low-key
    musical instruments

- [ ] toys
- [ ] diary & pencil
- [ ] binoculars
- [ ] watch
- [ ] thermometer
- [ ] even more books
- [ ] field guides (birds, insects, plants, mammals)

V. Hiking & Backpacking Checklist
(2–4 people)

Group Equipment

- [ ] stove/s (1 every 4 people)
- [ ] fuel for stove/s (1 qt/stove/day)
- [ ] pour spout or funnel for fuel
- [ ] 1 2-qt. & 1-qt. pots with lids (minimum list)
- [ ] coffee pot & lid
- [ ] frying pan & lid
- [ ] pliers or pot gripper
- [ ] mixing spoon & spatula
- [ ] lighter &/or lighter
- [ ] repair kit
- [ ] water filter
- [ ] water bladder or jug
- [ ] pot scrubber (nylon)
- [ ] biodegradable soap
- [ ] food bags

- [ ] food (enough for 3 meals/person/day)
- [ ] spice kit
- [ ] 2 @ 50' coils of lightweight nylon rope
- [ ] garbage bag
- [ ] tarp (waterproof)
- [ ] trowel
- [ ] toilet paper
- [ ] insect repellent
- [ ] sunscreen
- [ ] hand lotion
- [ ] candle lantern
- [ ] extra candles
- [ ] tents, poles, & tent stakes

Individual Equipment

- ☐ backpack
- ☐ day pack (optional)
- ☐ first-aid kit
- ☐ emergency food & shelter
- ☐ closed-cell foam pad (for sleeping)
- ☐ sleeping bag (and stuff sack)
- ☐ map/s
- ☐ compass
- ☐ whistle
- ☐ small pocket knife (adults only)
- ☐ water bottle
- ☐ cup, bowl, spoon, plate
- ☐ sunglasses
- ☐ towel or large bandana
- ☐ toothbrush & paste
- ☐ lip balm
- ☐ tampons or sanitary napkins
- ☐ sunglasses
- ☐ flashlight & extra batteries
- ☐ 50'—100' parachute cord
- ☐ small supply of toilet paper
- ☐ lighter &/or matches (adults only)

Individual Clothing (to wear & carry)

- ☐ hat with brim
- ☐ wool hat
- ☐ 2 pair underwear
- ☐ 2 T-shirts
- ☐ long johns (tops & bottoms)
- ☐ 4 pairs of wool socks
- ☐ gloves or mittens
- ☐ 1 pair shorts
- ☐ long wool or bunting pants
- ☐ long-sleeved wool or bunting shirt
- ☐ down vest or extra wool shirt
- ☐ sneakers
- ☐ lightweight trail boots
- ☐ gaiters
- ☐ raincoat & pants
- ☐ wind coat & pants

Optional Equipment

- ☐ sit pad
- ☐ books
- ☐ field guides
- ☐ fishing gear
- ☐ camera & film
- ☐ cards & games
- ☐ walking stick
- ☐ bear bell
- ☐ diary & pencil
- ☐ binoculars
- ☐ watch
- ☐ thermometer

VI. Sample Menu

Day	Breakfast	Lunch	Dinner
Wednesday	at home	bag lunch from home soda	hamburgers buns diced onions condiments pickles herb tea
Thursday	bacon eggs toast coffee tang	bagels salad cheese trail mix tea	spaghetti & sauce fresh biscuits packaged cheese cake herb tea
Friday	oatmeal milk raisins butter coffee tang	bannock peanut butter cheese trail mix tea	potato stew peas (dried) rice onions (fresh) tomatoes (dried) green beans (dried) herb tea
Saturday	granola powdered milk coffee tang	rye crisp cheese hard salami tea	macaroni & cheese peas (dried) instant pudding herb tea
Sunday	pancakes milk syrup tang coffee	bannock peanut butter cheese tea	at home

Spices (in small plastic jars or clean film canisters)
salt, pepper, dried onions, dried garlic, chili powder, parsley, basil, other spices you like.

VII. Minimum Impact Camping Quiz
Answer Key

Section 1: True/False Questions.

T $\boxed{F}$ It is a good idea to use brightly colored tents so your campsite can be easily spotted in an emergency.

In order to minimize your visual impacts (which affect other
campers' experiences) we recommend that you avoid bright colors whenever possible. If you're really worried about signaling for
a rescue, carry a brightly colored ground cloth, and only display it
when someone is trying to find you.

T $\boxed{F}$ One should burn and then bury used cans and other metal
containers.

Certainly not! Ideally, you won't have any cans or other metal containers with you on your trip, but if you do, you should wash
them with your dishes, flatten them, and carry them home to be
recycled.

T $\boxed{F}$ The size of a camping group is unimportant.

The size of the group is important, because it is a factor in the
amount of environmental degradation that will result from use of
a campsite, and it also affects the sociological impacts your group
will have on others. Keep groups as small as you can; outside
developed campgrounds, groups should never be more than ten
members, and should usually be no more than six.

$\boxed{T}$ F Meadows and grassy areas are usually the preferred place
to camp in a wilderness or primitive area.

Sometimes, anyway. Grassy meadows tend to be reasonably soft
and environmentally resilient—if you are only staying for a short
time and don't plan on building a fire. As long as your site is well

175

shielded by trees, plants, and/or geography, and isn't in a sensitive transitional environment, grass is generally more comfortable than a rock slab. We usually recommend the rock slabs anyway, though, because they are very hard to damage inadvertently.

$\boxed{T}$ F   To avoid excessive damage to the environment, stay no more than two days at one campsite.

In undeveloped campsites, two days is okay as long as you move your tents during the day so the biota under them get sunlight and air. Two nights and one day is, perhaps, a better "maximum" stay in undeveloped sites. For developed sites (in organized campgrounds), the maximum length of your stay can be determined by the length of your vacation, or campground rules and regulations.

T $\boxed{F}$ It's always a good idea to build a circle of stones to contain a campfire.

In fact, it is almost never a good idea to do so. If you must have a fire, it should be inside a metal grate (if one is provided) or in a fire pit.

$\boxed{T}$ F   A minimum impact site should be at least 200 feet from trails, lakes, streams, meadows, or scenic areas.

Two hundred feet is a good distance—it's close enough for you to go enjoy the scenery, but far enough away that other people can enjoy it, too.

T $\boxed{F}$ A cat-hole latrine should be dug in dry, sandy, or gravel soil, at least 50 feet from water, camp, or trails.

In areas where cat-hole latrines are permitted, they should be 150 to 200 feet away from the water, campsite, or trail, and should be in organic soil so the wastes decompose more quickly.

T $\boxed{F}$ Fish entrails should be tossed back into the lake or stream as food for turtles and other fish.

This one is tough to answer definitively because resource managers aren't all sold on a single "best" solution. When regulations permit it, entrails should be buried in organic soil well away from a campsite, trail, or water source, otherwise they should be packed out with the garbage.

T $\boxed{F}$ Loud games and campfire programs are appropriate camping activities for large groups.

Considering their impact on other groups (and their potential impact on nervous wildlife), loud games are best saved for home. Campfire "programs" are okay if they're quiet, but, all things considered, they're better off being candle-lantern programs.

T $\boxed{F}$ If conditions are muddy, it is a good idea to walk parallel to the established trail.

If you walk next to a muddy trail, there will soon be two muddy trails next to each other. Boots can be cleaned and so can feet, so it is a good idea to minimize impacts by staying on the trail even if it is muddy. Step carefully, though, to avoid slipping.

T $\boxed{F}$ It is good etiquette to leave a pile of wood for the next user of a primitive site.

Many of the people who travel in primitive or undeveloped areas want to get the feeling that no one else has been in their site for years. If you have leftover wood, it is, therefore, better to scatter it in the woods surrounding the site than it is to pile it. Besides, you probably shouldn't have a fire anyway.

T $\boxed{F}$ Rules don't apply in the wilderness.

Of course they do!

Section 2: Other Questions:

Q. Beside hanging your food pack properly, what is the best way
  to avoid problems with bears at your site?

  Keep the campsite so clean that the bears aren't interested
  in it.

Q. Why should you wear lightweight shoes at your campsite?

  The lighter your shoes, the less damage you'll do to the soil,
  plants, and insects you walk on. Also, light shoes will generally
  keep your legs and feet happier than heavy boots.

Q. What key words describe the most appropriate type of wood
  for use in your cooking fire?

  "We don't use fires," "we brought wood from home," or "we
  purchased it at the camp store" are probably the best answers.
  If you collect your own wood, though, down, dead, dry, and distant should describe its condition. The "rule of thumb" should
  describe its size.

Q. What is the best way to dispose of food scraps?

  Eat them. If you can't stomach that, pack them out in your
  garbage bag.

Q. Describe an ideal tent site.

  We both like nice, almost level areas that are naturally free
  from large stones, tree roots, branches, and assorted lumps. An
  ideal site is also clear of any large branches or trees that might
  fall during a storm and isn't in a depression. A slight incline
  doesn't hurt, if you expect rain, because it can drain water
  away from your tent.

Q. Why should you not build fires directly on the ground?

  Because they leave scars (which are a sociological impact) and
  because they can set the duff (or top layer of soil) on fire result-
  ing in all sorts of environmental damage.

Q. Is bark peeled from a live birch tree a good form of tinder?

No! Never peel bark from a live tree. It can damage or kill the tree, and doesn't look very nice, either.

Q. How can you tell if your fire is completely out?

Feel it with your hand. We know it's messy, but it does work. If you can feel any warm spots, use more water.

Q. Describe the best procedure for washing anything (including yourself) with soap in a wilderness area.

The best answer is, "Don't use soap." The real one, for those of you who have social needs, is to wash with biodegradable soap at least 150 feet away from any lake, stream, or wetland so the soap ends up in the soil, where it can biodegrade. Never use soap directly in the water, or use it in a place that will allow suds to drain directly into the water.

Q. Describe a no-trace check.

The group leader personally checks every campsite or rest area after use to eliminate all traces of the group's use of the site. This includes erasing fire scars, closing latrines, replacing moved objects, collecting all the litter (especially tent stakes and twist ties), filling the sump hole, scattering leftover fire wood, and generally making the site as pristine as possible.

Q. How large an axe is required for safe camping?

This is a trick question. Leave the axe at home!

Q. What does "take nothing but pictures, leave nothing but foot-prints" mean?

Exactly what it says. Minimize your impacts by leaving the places you visit untouched (or as untouched as possible) by your presence. If you "take nothing but pictures" and "leave nothing but footprints" no one will ever know you've been camping (which is good) until you show them the pictures after dinner (which can be even better).